THE SECRET OF THE THOTH TAROT

THE SECRET OF THE THOTH TAROT

The Origins of Aleister Crowley's
Book of Thoth

Paul Hughes-Barlow

XX_III_MMXXV

AEON

British Library Cataloguing in Publication Data

A C.I.P. for this book is available from the British Library

ISBN-13: 978-1-80152-189-5

Typeset by Medlar Publishing Solutions Pvt Ltd, India

www.aeonbooks.co.uk

CONTENTS

PART FIVE: CONCLUSIONS

APPENDIX

ACKNOWLEDGEMENTS

I extend my deepest gratitude to Master Pundit Joshi and Pundit Maharaj, whose lineage as astrologers to the Maharajas of India spans centuries. Their blessings and unparalleled spiritual wisdom have been invaluable in shaping this work.

I am deeply grateful for the invaluable assistance and expertise of the librarians at the Museum of Freemasonry.

Bart Deleplanque deserves heartfelt thanks for his inspiration, encouragement, and unwavering support. His collaboration in creating videos on the *Book of Thoth* and his contributions to my Facebook group have been instrumental. His keen insights into the Roman numerals of the Atu have illuminated many aspects of this journey.

A special thanks to my Founding Patrons on patreon.com/paulhughesbarlow. Your belief in my work and generous support have made this book possible.

Finally, I am profoundly grateful to my publisher for their patience and faith in me. Their steadfast belief that I would deliver something—anything—sustained me, even as the process took far longer than anticipated.

FOREWORD

by Bart Deleplanque

The resplendent journey of the Thoth Tarot

It is with immense honour and delight that I introduce this masterful work by my dear friend, Paul Hughes-Barlow. Over the past years, I have had the privilege of collaborating with Paul on numerous projects centred around the Thoth Tarot, including a series of in-depth YouTube videos and workshops. Our shared passion for the Thoth Tarot has not only strengthened our friendship but has also deepened my appreciation for the profound wisdom and transformative power encapsulated within this unique Tarot deck.

Paul Hughes-Barlow is no stranger to the esoteric world. As an esteemed Taro card reader and scholar from Brighton, UK, his previous work, *The Tarot and the Magus*, has already carved out its place as a classic within the niche genre of Thoth Tarot literature. With this new book, Paul embarks on a journey through the history and background of the *Book of Thoth*, the enigmatic Society of Eight, and the use of tarot for invocation. The bar is set high, but I have no doubt that Paul's intricate knowledge, coupled with his profound respect for the subject, will meet and exceed all expectations.

Unearthing the history of the Book of Thoth

In this new book, Paul delves into the rich tapestry of the *Book of Thoth*, unearthing its historical roots and the myriad influences that have shaped its evolution. The Thoth Tarot, conceived by Aleister Crowley and illustrated by Frieda Harris, is much more than a mere deck of cards. It is a labyrinth of symbols, each meticulously chosen to convey layers of meaning, hidden and apparent.

Paul's exploration of the *Book of Thoth* transcends a simple recounting of its history. He guides readers through the complex web of esoteric traditions and organisations that have contributed to its formation. Each chapter unfolds like a ritual, revealing the intricacies of the symbols and the profound teachings they encapsulate.

The approach is both scholarly and accessible. He provides a comprehensive overview of the historical and philosophical contexts that have shaped the *Book of Thoth*, making this work an invaluable resource for both novices and seasoned practitioners. His ability to distil complex ideas into clear, engaging prose is a testament to his expertise and his passion for sharing the Mysteries of the Thoth Tarot with a wider audience.

The Society of Eight: guardians of the esoteric tradition

One of the most intriguing aspects of this book is Paul's examination of the Society of Eight, a lesser known but highly influential group within the esoteric community. The Society of Eight has played a crucial role in shaping the teachings of the Thoth Tarot, and Paul's in-depth research sheds light on their contributions and their enduring legacy.

Through meticulous research and insightful analysis, Paul unveils the secrets of the Society of Eight, exploring the profound influence they have had on the development of modern esoteric traditions. This exploration is not merely academic; it is an invitation to the reader to delve deeper into the Mysteries of the Thoth Tarot and to engage with its teachings on a personal and transformative level.

Paul's portrayal of the Society of Eight is both respectful and revelatory. He honours their contributions while also challenging readers to consider the broader implications of their work for contemporary esoteric practice. This balance of reverence and critical inquiry is a hallmark of Paul's writing and is sure to resonate with readers who are seeking a deeper understanding of the Thoth Tarot and its place within the broader esoteric tradition.

The tarot as a tool for invocation

Perhaps the most compelling aspect of Paul's new book is his exploration of the use of tarot for invocation. While the Thoth Tarot is often used for divination, Paul emphasises its potential as a tool for spiritual initiation and transformation. He explores the ways in which the cards can be used to invoke specific energies, deities, and archetypes, providing readers with practical techniques for incorporating tarot into their own spiritual practice.

Paul's approach to tarot invocation is both innovative and grounded in tradition. He draws on his extensive knowledge of esoteric practices, including alchemy, witchcraft, and sex magick, to offer a comprehensive guide to using the Thoth Tarot as a tool for personal and spiritual growth. His insights into the symbolic language of the cards and their connections to various esoteric traditions provide readers with a rich and multifaceted understanding of the Thoth Tarot's potential as a tool for invocation.

In this book, Paul challenges readers to go beyond the surface meanings of the cards and to engage with their deeper symbolic and spiritual significance through three new spreads: ABRAHADABRA, Vision of 231, and 6° = 5°. He invites readers to explore the hidden realms of the Thoth Tarot and to use these powerful systems as Keys to unlock new levels of consciousness and understanding. This approach is both empowering and transformative, offering readers a new way of engaging with the Thoth Tarot that goes beyond traditional divination.

A testament to friendship and shared passion

My journey with Paul began at a Thoth Tarot workshop, and our shared passion for this remarkable deck has only deepened over time. Through countless discussions, workshops, and video projects, we have explored the many facets of the Thoth Tarot, from its historical roots to its practical applications. Our friendship is a testament to the power of shared passion and the transformative potential of the Thoth Tarot.

Paul's dedication to his craft and his unwavering commitment to sharing his knowledge with others is evident in every page of this book.

His writing is infused with a deep respect for the traditions he explores and a genuine desire to help others unlock the Mysteries of the Thoth Tarot. It is an honour to call him a friend and a privilege to introduce this important new work to a wider audience.

In conclusion, I am confident that Paul Hughes-Barlow's new book will become an essential resource for anyone interested in the Thoth Tarot, its history, and its potential as a tool for spiritual invocation. It is a work that reflects the depth of Paul's knowledge, the breadth of his research, and his unwavering passion for the esoteric traditions that have shaped the Thoth Tarot. I am excited to see how this book will inspire and transform its readers, just as Paul's work has inspired and transformed me.

Bart Deleplanque
12 June 2024
Oudenburg, Belgium

PREFACE

How Aleister Crowley expressed his Will (Thelema) in creating the *Book of Thoth* in preparation for the New Aeon as foretold by the *Book of the Law*.

The TARO: Gateway to the Universe

The TARO is a *Map of the Universe*. The *Book of Thoth*, co-authored by Tahuti and Frater Perdurabo, serves as both the guide and the means to navigate this cosmic map. Designed as a manual of invocation for the students of the A∴A∴—an order established in 1907 for personal spiritual development—the *Book of Thoth* guides the aspirant from the First Order through the Portal to the Second Order, culminating in the attainment of Adeptus Minor 5° = 6°. The *Book of Thoth* charts the aspirant's journey toward becoming a Magus 9° = 2°, the pinnacle of mastery, the Great Work.

The modern Lineage of Masters begins with Martinez de Pasqually, Jean-Marie Ragon, Eliphas Levi, Kenneth Mackenzie, Frederick Holland, R.W. Little, Frederick Hockley, F.G. Irwin, W.W. Westcott, John Yarker, Benjamin Cox, Allan Bennett, George Cecil Jones, Oscar Eckenstein, Dion Fortune, Martha Küntzel, and Frieda Harris.

The *Book of Thoth* inspires students to progress from foundational knowledge of Magick and Mysticism to a deeper engagement with the writings of Aleister Crowley and other luminaries, including Tahuti, Lillith, Lola, John the Baptist, Mary Magdelene, the Virgin Mary, Jesus Christ, John of Patmos, Gautama Buddha, William Shakespeare, Christian Rosenkreutz, Lao Tse, Fu Hsi, John Dee, Edward Kelley, and Cagliostro.

Step onto the sacred path mapped by the *Book of Thoth*—a gateway to spiritual mastery and cosmic understanding. Whether you're an aspirant seeking the wisdom of the A∴A∴ or a student of esoteric traditions, this profound manual offers the Keys to navigate the *Map of the Universe*.

Join the lineage of Seekers and Masters who have dared to explore the Mysteries, from Pasqually to Frieda Harris, and let their wisdom guide your journey. Through the TARO, ascend from foundational knowledge to the heights of spiritual attainment, unlocking the teachings of Aleister Crowley and Tahuti.

TARO ROTA TORA ATOR

The Supreme Secret is not sex magick, a secret word, or a particular ritual. None of the modern secret societies hold the true Keys to Magick. If there is a Supreme Secret, it is the value and importance of the tarot that is central to mysticism and magick. Thus far, this secret is easy to keep, for modern-day secret societies continue to denigrate the importance of the tarot to the point of an irrelevance. The truth is that Aleister Crowley inherited the tarot and its significance while in the Golden Dawn. His obsession, shared with the Masters, is in his writings and diaries. The secret is kept simply by ignoring historical facts and writing historical narratives expunged of references to the tarot. Ignore the tarot and it will go away.

Today, all the Ordo Templis Orientis (O.T.O.) has to say on the *Book of Thoth* is the transposition of The Emperor with The Star, as if that is the only thing of interest that need concern students. Of course, there is no resolution or solution to this conundrum, a distraction which suits everyone concerned.

Suppressing the true nature of the tarot is achieved by distorting our view of Aleister Crowley to the point where he is a one-dimensional cartoon character obsessed with social climbing and cooking curry for Frieda Harris. While it might be revelatory to modern-day readers that Crowley met so many people, the reason why we did not know is because these people were never important to Crowley in the first place, and so he did not record them. Such irrelevant tittle-tattle is demeaning, but it sells books and promotes the cult of personality over knowledge.

Historically, the O.T.O. has never had any interest in the tarot, but that does not stop it from suppressing scholastic study of it. Aleister Crowley ran the O.T.O. until his death and never named a successor, for he knew the ambitions, character defects, and flaws of the candidates, and more importantly, their lack of interest in the tarot. All the more galling then, that he wrote, edited, and published the *Book of Thoth*, effectively by-passing the O.T.O. and continuing his own legacy and transmission of the secret knowledge of the tarot. Outsmarted, all the O.T.O. can do is continue lip service and pocket the income from the book.

It is an open secret amongst the elite of these esoteric groups that from the beginning of his magickal quest, Aleister Crowley habitually uses "Rota" when referring to the taro. However, in this book I use taro, which is still a radical departure for many tarot students. When reading "taro", please read it silently as Rota. Silence preserves the power of Rota. Otherwise, Tarot is devoid of power.

Circularity is found in the four-fold process of the Tetragrammaton fulfilled in the fifth element, Spirit, also expressed as Geburah, Mars, the pentagram, or the Sphinx. The *Book of Thoth* is a complex spinning circle that always returns us to a source, expressed in many forms found throughout Crowley's writings, some of which are explored in this book. As an example, let us investigate the forms of Rota with *Olla*, Crowley's last book, a selection of poems written throughout his life. Superficially there is no connection between the two, except that Olla and Rota are forms of YHVH which presents intriguing possibilities for further exploration.

The *Book of Thoth* is the *summum bonum* of Crowley's life; the very title is ambiguous, for the name originates in Ancient Egypt. Despite all the talk of the New Age, Crowley is telling us to look to the past for the truth. Thoth, or Tahuti, is Mercury, the trickster, the messenger of the Gods, a Divine Being, and a liar—Crowley wrote the *Book of Lies*. Lies are truths and vice versa—it all depends on perspective and levels of consciousness. The Master cannot communicate the truth to the student in a way that can be comprehended easily. Jesus spoke in parables.

TARO expressed in English, Greek or Hebrew give different gematria values. All are valid; the problem is that it is not always clear which version Crowley intends, particularly when he mixes the languages without telling you! For example, the final O of Taro can be expressed as 0, the letter O, which can refer to Atu O, The Fool, or Atu XV, The Devil. The T can be Teth, Lust, or it can be Tau, the last letter of the Hebrew alphabet. The last is first, and the first is last. Playing the game further, Aleph is the letter associated with Atu 0, so we have two Fools in Rota, perfect duality expressed as 0 = 2 or 2 = 0. There are many circular expressions in the *Book of Thoth*, which is apt when we consider the TARO to be the wheel, never stationary. When Crowley writes of the whirling motion of the Taro, he may be referring to the first word of Genesis; to the writings of Zoroaster; the 20th Aethyr KHR; or the swastika, transformed by the Nazis into a symbol of evil, upon which Crowley had to remain silent.

Pronunciation and phonetics are fertile grounds for layers of ambiguity and nuance which Crowley weaves between real people in his life, symbolism and the taro; the best example of which is Lola.

Lola Zaza (1906–1990) is Crowley's second daughter. Lola is the Key of Delights in *The Wake World* (1907). On the 22nd of December 1946 (the Winter Solstice), Aleister Crowley published his final book, a selection of his poems in a book named *Olla*, another anagram. Laylah is the Arabic form of "night", linked to ALLH, Allah. The number of Laylah is 77 immortalised in the *Book of Lies*, Chapter 77, one less than the number of cards in a tarot deck. The following chapter, "Wheel and—Whoa!" is included in the *Book of Thoth* without commentary. The lily, a symbol of purity, is the fleur-de-lys which appears on both the Emperor and Empress cards. Finally, Leila Waddel (1880–1932), an Australian, and a talented violinist, was Crowley's Scarlet Woman and revered as the "Mother of Heaven".

Lola activates Taro through ADNY, from neutrality to masculinity, while the magician invokes Thoth daily. Male and female in their simplest forms are the union of I and O. The Divine Name IAO is the Triune form of YHVH, the mysteries of which form a powerful system of magick using the Taro.

Aiwass dictated this short but vitally important chapter on the permutations in the correct order. ORAT, to speak, is no longer silent: it has a Voice that spins the Wheel. Rota and Olla form magickal equations which for the moment must remain silent.

Separating the man, magician, mystic, and mythology of Aleister Crowley from the Taro is an impossible task.

BERASHITH

This is the Magical History
Of the Dawning of the Light.
Begun are the Whirling Motions;
Formulated is the Primal Fire;
Proclaimed is the Reign of the Gods of Light
At the Threshold of the Infinite Worlds!

(Berashith, 1903)

Understanding this enigmatic book requires abandoning every thought and idea of what the tarot is about until one starts to think the way Aleister Crowley does. That is when the magic happens.

> *He succeeded in uniting under the Holy Qabalah, of which the Tarot is*
> *he greatest single element, all philosophical and magical systems soever,*
> *including that of the Chinese.*
>
> (Bibliographical Note in the *Book of Thoth*)

This sounds like hyperbole, even when he speaks in the third person, but it turns out to be a true statement. How he did this requires listening to his voice rather than the supposed adherents and experts with all their agendas and propaganda who know his system more than he does. Blanking out the noise and blather around this man requires a superhuman effort. Fortunately, he gives techniques for dealing with this in the *Book of the Law*, but we are getting ahead of ourselves.

To know all these systems requires extensive study outside of the *Book of Thoth*. Fortunately, Crowley writes eloquently on all of them.

The modern publishing history of Aleister Crowley's life has become a relentless soap opera of name-dropping which is all very interesting but tells us nothing of his magical and philosophical systems, which is, no doubt, the purpose of the exercise.

Another purpose is to gently lead the student away from the stress of reading *The Confessions of Aleister Crowley*. Most people give up before getting even a quarter of the way through this book, which is a shame, for amongst other things we get to learn when the *Book of Thoth* was written. The ambiguity of the prose style means that it can be confusing as to what Crowley is writing about, no doubt compounded by elements of confusion in the editors John Symonds and Kenneth Grant, who evidently fell out at some point. Reading *Confessions* is tough, a literary boot camp whose themes help us to glimpse the clues which will lead us, in Crowley's words, to the goal of the Tarot.

The Confessions delivers the context of Crowley's life as it relates to the Tarot amongst other things, in particular his involvement in MacGregor Mathers' Hermetic Order of the Golden Dawn, which was less than two years of his life. Mathers never had contact with the Hidden Masters, which is his greatest crime as far Crowley was concerned. Undeterred, Crowley had already embarked on more fruitful lines of enquiry—the *Book of the Sacred Magick of Abramelin the Mage*, translated by Mathers, ironically, inspired him to purchase Boleskine, which would also be a base for mountaineering. He was also hosting ritual magic sessions with George Cecil Jones and Allan Bennett at his flat in Holborn.

After the grand expulsion, Mathers directed Crowley to travel to Mexico to find more followers (in reality to get Crowley away from discovering the truth about his misdemeanours). While there, Crowley became a 33° Mason (Freemasonry was influential throughout his life) and he established his first Temple of *LIL*, whose rituals contained elements of the *Cipher Manuscript* and prayers written by Eliphas Levi.

The *Cipher Manuscript* and *Book T* are the foundations of Mather's Golden Dawn (GD), which originated from the Society of Eight. These books are the foundation for the A∴A∴ founded in 1907 and expounded further in *The Equinox* books. The basis of the *Book of Thoth* is the *Cipher Manuscript* and *Book T* which places it within the tradition of the Society of Eight.

In the meantime, Abra-melin spirits informed Crowley that he was under attack from Mathers, whose martial energy was persistently problematic. In order to completely break the link with Mathers and to initiate his own system based upon *Book T* and the *Cipher Manuscript*, Crowley travelled to Egypt to perform his own rituals to initiate the new Magical Current. *Liber AL* was lost until Crowley found it again five years later while looking for a painting of the Water Watchtower at Boleskine. This serendipity led Crowley to Tunisia to complete his journey through the 30 Aethyrs.

Even after Mathers' death, the problems continued, requiring Crowley to perform the banishing rituals in the Cephaelodium Working at Cefalù.

This, in a nutshell, is the background to the *Book of Thoth*, whose genesis is with the Society of Eight. The study of this book requires extensive study of Crowley's system, which basically means studying everything he wrote which is relevant. Turning the topic on its head, the *Book of Thoth* is Crowley's key to understanding all his writings including the *Book of the Law*.

PART ONE

AN INTRODUCTION TO THE
BOOK OF THOTH

CHAPTER ONE

How to study the *Book of Thoth*

A leister Crowley designed the *Book of Thoth* so that students have to diligently study and cross-reference his extensive mystical and magical literature as well as other writers on the subject. There is a caveat: before you rush out to increase your library, make sure you purchase his original texts, not the modern versions that have been doctored or 'edited, improved, mistakes corrected'. Most 'mistakes' were deliberately included by Crowley as silent markers to alert the reader to pay attention and explore deeper.

Rather than mentally tut-tutting at Crowley's howlers, make a note for reference. Soon you will be actively looking for mistakes. The secret to reading Aleister Crowley is to avoid modern versions that have been 'corrected'.

Aleister Crowley demands that the student thinks for herself and be confident in her new thoughts and insights, not minding that these insights are fleeting when new research quashes or contradicts those thoughts, often for months or years. These irritants are the fuel and inspiration to continue research. Rather than sit on the fence, it is better to make a conclusion, however half-baked, crazy, or inaccurate, for to make this declaration sets in train forces that will reveal new knowledge, aspects of the knowledge, or a direct contradiction. Friends got used to my daily contradictions on the current state of play.

This is the method to unlock the secrets of the *Book of Thoth*. These insights concatenate and accelerate in a non-linear manner—there is no beginning or end, no optimum narrative. This is the inner process of *solve et coagula* at work. Writing this book is in part an expression of my own inner journey that will continue long after it is published.

The original idea for this book was to write footnotes; an exercise that took months before I admitted failure. At the same time I was correcting mistakes in Crowley's text! After many failures, and false starts the decision was taken to focus on the history and background that gives context to Crowley's life and his place in the history of the TARO. Future books will delve into the individual cards.

The true key to opening The Book of Thoth

The *Book of Thoth* remains forever closed to the student while she pursues the three main red herrings. The publishing date of 1944 is a dead end, while the previous years from 1938 when Aleister Crowley met Frieda Harris provides no clues. Equally useless is the O.T.O. favourite, that of the transposition of The Star with The Emperor found in the *Book of the Law* in 1904. The O.T.O. is particularly obsessed about the transposition to the point that the only thing of interest is the transposition in the *Book of Thoth*. Far better to consider that a number significant to The Star is found in the Magic Square of Mars and the Svastika.

The Key to opening the *Book of Thoth* is in the 'History' section which covers the tumultuous years of the Hermetic Order of the Golden Dawn culminating in the expulsion of its leader, Samuel Liddell MacGregor Mathers in January 1900 for the fraudulent actions surrounding Frau Sprengel when the Order was formed. Ever since the Order has tied itself in knots over this issue, which we will examine later. As we know, Mathers' protégé, Aleister Crowley, was also evicted at the same as several other members.

We would expect such an expulsion to be devastating to Crowley, but that is not the case, for it was the making of him and the seed for *Liber AL*.

The whole Sprengel affair is a side-show to cover up a greater scandal, at least in Crowley's eyes. Ever since reading *Zanoni* by Bullwer Lytton, Crowley was obsessed with meeting the Secret Chiefs, which lead him to be introduced into the Golden Dawn. It is the duty of the leaders of secret societies to make contact with the Hidden Masters, and Crowley believed that Mathers had achieved this.

One paragraph is telling:

> *Shortly afterwards, Mathers, who had manoeuvred himself into the prac-tical Headship of the Order, announced that he had made this link; that the Secret Chiefs had authorized him to continue the work of the Order, as its sole head. There is, however, no evidence that he was here a wit-ness of truth, because no new knowledge of any particular importance came to the Order; such as did appear proved to be no more than Mathers could have acquired by normal means from quite accessible sources, such as the British Museum. These circumstances, and a great deal of petty intrigue, led to serious dissatisfaction among the members of the Order. Frl. Sprengel's judgment, that group-working in an Order of this sort is possible, was shown in this case to be wrong. In 1900, the Order in its existing form was destroyed.*
>
> (*Book of Thoth*)

Supporters of Mathers gloss over his inability to make the link. Without such a link, the Order has no validity, which did not of course stop the GD continuing in numerous forms by those who also had no link to the Hidden Chiefs. This tradition continues to this day.

Crowley has no problem with the Fräulein Sprengel debacle, for almost all magical orders make entirely implausible claims to their origins—its par for the course. He continued to be loyal to Mathers after the expulsion, for he went on an expedition to Mexico to establish a new temple on Mathers behalf.

By now, Crowley was obsessed with the Tarot as well as the Hidden Masters, and he was determined to find the truth, however long it took, and whatever it takes. In Crowley's world, Tarot and Hidden Masters become interchangeable terms.

There are two other memes that cloud judgement and impede prog-ress on the *Book of Thoth*. The first meme is the inclusion of GD mate-rial on the Tarot. Apart from the 'History' section, no Golden Dawn related material is to be found—this was a difficult one for me. Since neither Mathers nor the other founders had the magical link to the Hidden Masters, it follows that all teachings of the Golden Dawn are null and void. When the penny dropped for me, I instantly lost interest in reading Golden Dawn books.

The second meme is the influence of O.T.O. on the *Book of Thoth*. There is in truth very little relevance to the O.T.O., despite Crowley's copious references to *Liber AL* which serve another purpose.

While the leaders of subsequent Golden Dawn and O.T.O. organisations conveniently abandoned the notion of linking to the Secret Chiefs, they were not stupid, and if they had read the *Book of Thoth*, they too understood Crowley's position and decided to ignore it. No wonder this book and Crowley are hated so much.

Foundations of the Book of Thoth

Crowley set himself two tasks, one to make the link to the Hidden Masters and provide proof, which he did with *Liber AL*.

The second task was to discover the practical magical and mystical origins of the Tarot. This task was relatively simple, for Crowley had already come across the relevant documents while a member of the GD! The roots of the *Book of Thoth* is found in these documents:

- *Cipher Manuscript*
- *Book T*
- *Vision of the Universal Mercury*

All three documents are part of Mather's GD system, so why include them despite the absence of GD materiel in the *Book of Thoth*? The answer is simple, Mathers appropriated the documents from elsewhere.

The authorship of all three documents is open to question—it certainly wasn't Mathers. It is safe to say that Crowley found out where these documents originated.

Why was Crowley supremely confident he would achieve his goals? The clues are in activities at the same time as his progress in the GD. When not mountaineering or openly exploring his bisexuality, Crowley had already embarked on an ambitious spiritual and magical programme. He was progressing through the stages of Freemasonry (more of which later); he purchased Boleskine in Scotland to pursue the Abra-melin ritual (based ironically on Mathers' translation); he rented a flat in Holborn where he ritually invoked the Goetia with the two best magicians in the GD, George Cecil Jones and Allan Bennett.

Just one of these magical activities is enough to overload the system— no one in their right mind would recommend it—while it is almost impossible to attribute which system contributed most to his magical and spiritual growth, we can safely assume that the Abra-melin workings were core, as Abra-melin would continue to work throughout the rest of his life.

Astral attacks

With all these activities it is no wonder that Crowley bounced back from the disappointment and disillusionment of Mathers' mendacity. Furthermore, the true nature of Mathers was revealed in Crowley's magical workings with Abra-melin and the Goetia, when he realised Mathers was attacking him astrally, probably from the end of 1900 onwards at various times. In other words, Mathers was a black magician. Crowley was not the only 'victim' of Mathers evil intent.

Astral attacks might sound shocking, but they are very commonplace. No need for a ritual—all that is required is constant negative thoughts directed towards the victim. Sometimes the attacker is known to the victim, but often not. In either case, the attack can be subtle and therefore undetected, or it can be more aggressive. If someone comes into your mind, it can simply suggest they are thinking about you, which can be reassuring, or it can be more sinister. Practical experience and an open mind is key to knowing the difference.

We all know someone who constantly obsesses about another person.

This is going to sound strange, but while attacks are not exactly to be welcomed, they are very useful for research purposes. An attack is often a sign of progress in the right direction that is being blocked. The author had many such experiences that had to be overcome while writing this book. Attacks are always an opportunity for intelligence gathering, the who, what, why, where, and most importantly how the action was taken. In my experience most attacks are almost always never demonic—they are man-made. When a demon attacks, it is usually a cry for help from the demon, who wants to be released from its obligation, who in return will help his liberator.

To know, to dare, to will, and keep silent

Magical attacks do not require a ritual—it is the intent that counts. It is not a requirement that the attacker even knows what he or she is doing. It is possible to absolutely believe in one's own good nature and intent, and still practice black magic.

My definition of black magic is action or intent designed to make the victim deviate or not find their true nature. Crowley's intense desire to meet the Hidden Masters or Secret Chiefs create shockwaves in the ether picked up by friends and foes alike creating a classic battle between good and evil, where the Secret Chiefs silently assist the aspirant towards the goal, while the enemies work to block progress.

In Crowley's case, the Secret Chiefs led him to join the Golden Dawn knowing Mathers' true nature. When expelled, it is more than likely that Crowley saw this as an intervention from the Secret Chiefs, and Crowley knew the methods used by Mathers because he had studied Mathers translation of Abra-melin.

By getting expelled, the Hidden Masters were directing Crowley towards the right path—how else would he have known about the *Cipher Manuscript, Book T,* or the *Vision of the Universal Mercury?*

We do not know when Crowley discovered who was behind these documents, but it is quite possible that he knew of them from his Masonic connections. Either way, he named the candidates in the *Book of Thoth* that allows us to follow in his footsteps.

These clues are Eliphas Levi, Kenneth Mackenzie, John Yarker, and the Masonic organisations of the Societas Rosicruciana in Anglia (SRIA) and Quatuor Coronati.

CHAPTER TWO

The *Book of Thoth* in Masonry

The *Book of Thoth* is a manual for Master Masons who adhere to the ethos and propagation of the Society of Eight.

Here is the reason why this book is so difficult to read. This secret was withheld from Frieda Harris as she worked on the designs. Aleister Crowley kept this secret while he was studying the Tarot ever since he joined the Hermetic Order of the Golden Dawn in 1898. This secret is maintained when he wrote and published books on the Tarot.

Certain adepts within the O.T.O. also know this secret, and are determined to keep it that way. In 2006 I met one of these adepts in a London bookshop. In response to an innocent question on the *Book of Thoth*, his face contorted, telling me that 'Crowley was old, decrepit, dying, sick, on drugs etc., etc.'. The implication being that he was *non compos mentis* for the time he was working with Frieda Harris. Perhaps the Nazi bombs drove him crazy. This vile trashing of the man who he was supposed to venerate shocked me. It was also the moment I determined to discover why he made that extraordinary statement.

The O.T.O. have a problem, for while they make money from sales of the book (most important!) the priority is to prevent serious academic research ever taking place. Fortunately for the O.T.O., most magicians treat the *Book of Thoth* as an irrelevance, but there is always the danger that a tarot student gets above himself and asks dangerous (for the O.T.O.) questions.

The O.T.O. tightly controls access to Crowley's manuscripts, and only researchers and historians trusted to hold the party line are permitted to publish, their manuscripts having had prior approval before publishing. There is no such thing as independent research when it comes to getting O.T.O. approval. Fortunately for us all the clues needed to reach the conclusion about the Society of Eight are found in the *Book of Thoth* with corroborating evidence from Masonic Libraries.

The problem for the O.T.O. is that Crowley was always one step ahead, for clues are scattered within his published works such as *The Equinox*, the *Book of Lies*, *Confessions of Aleister Crowley*, *777*, and yes, even *Liber AL*. The *Book of Thoth* is the culmination of his efforts. This ultra-secret project needed to be discovered by students of the tarot who are as passionate as the Master Masons who formed the Society of Eight in the first place. Better late than never.

The first line of defence is the statement 'the *Book of Thoth* was published in 1944'. While this is obviously true, the reader naturally assumes that the book was written during the period from 1938 to 1944 when Crowley worked with Frieda Harris. Crowley seemed to anticipate this when he wrote in the 'Bibliographical Note':

> He published a full account of the Tarot, according to the MSS. of the Hermetic Order of the Golden Dawn in The Equinox, Vol I, Nos 7 and 9 (1912 e.v.).
>
> During all this time the Tarot was his daily companion, guide, and object of research.
>
> (Bibliographical Note in the Book of Thoth)

Crowley confirmed this research was completed in Cefalù, 1920–1922, when he says:

> The true significance of the Atus of Tahuti, or Tarot Trumps, also awaits full understanding. I have satisfied myself that these twenty-two cards compose a complete system of hieroglyphs representing the total energies of the Universe. In the case of some cards, I have succeeded in restoring the original form and giving a complete account of their meaning. Others, however, I understand imperfectly, and of some few I have at present obtained no more than a general idea.
>
> (The Confessions of Aleister Crowley)

Clearly these gaps were filled before and during his collaboration with Frieda Harris. Note:

> *I have succeeded in restoring the original form and giving a complete account of their meaning.*
>
> COMMENTARY
>
> *He succeeded in uniting under the Schema of the Holy Qabalah, of which the Tarot is the greatest single element, all philosophical and magical systems whatsoever, including that of the Chinese. This, and his 'Naples Arrangement' are with little doubt his greatest achievements in scholarship.*
>
> (Bibliographical Note in the *Book of Thoth*)

The natural assumption is that the O.T.O. are the custodians of this knowledge, who would like it kept secret. Unfortunately, this line of reasoning results in a dead end, unless of course the O.T.O. proves otherwise. The problem for the O.T.O. is that historically this organisation has never taken an interest in the Tarot.

Freemasons as custodians of the Tarot?

The grade structure and teachings of Freemasonry reveals no mention of Tarot, while it is rare for a tarot student to have knowledge of Masonry. The Hermetic Order of the Golden Dawn is often described as quasi-Masonic, but since it is seen as a level above Freemasonry, there is no need to study the basics.

As a result, the numerous Masonic references in the *Book of Thoth* are easily ignored or dismissed.

CHAPTER THREE

An overview of *The Book of Thoth*

Aleister Crowley is synonymous with black magic, yet I found myself scrabbling to comprehend the profound ethical moral philosophy of Immanuel Kant, whose philosophical terms appear in several places. It was a bigger shock to discover that Kant influenced Crowley throughout his life from around 1900 at the latest. Do we find Kant in the *Book of the Law*? Indeed we do.

Perhaps Kant should be taught to budding magicians and tarot students alike in secret societies? It was in Crowley's A∴A∴.

Bart Deleplanque's powerful vision of the Roman numerals is fascinating. *The Roman Numbers of the Trumps* gives clues as to its importance for The Fool as 0, and the transposition of Tzaddi in the *Book of the Law*.

Certain pages of the *Book of Thoth* stand out. Page 4 is critical to understanding its relevance, not just from the gematria, but as a central pillar of speculative Freemasonry. Page 10 has cryptic clues to the entire system, and the complementary diagrams on page 11, fulfilled on page 12. If that suggests to you Crowley combined gematria with page numbers, you would be correct.

The 'History' section is small, less than ten pages, and it is critical to understanding Crowley's knowledge of the TARO. Few students ever read this section, but it the missing piece to Crowley's experiences and account of Mathers' Golden Dawn, so I have included his other writings on the subject.

The 'History' section exposes the reader to Freemasonry, particularly the SRIA, Quatuor Coronati, and the Society of Eight. The origin of the Golden Dawn is Masonic. Mathers' books on the tarot are perfunctory and totally lacking in inspiration; while he butchered the *Cipher Manuscript* and *Book T* in the Tarot section of the big yellow book.

The GD attitude to the tarot explains why the *Book of Thoth* is so difficult to understand. Looked at from the other direction, knowing the *Book of Thoth* makes it easy to comprehend Mather's entire system, not just the tarot, and spot the many flaws. If you want to understand the flaws of Mather's GD, read the *Book of Thoth*.

Working from source material is critical, but here Crowley faced the same problem as the modern researcher. *Book T* and the *Cipher Manuscript* are the foundation, but there are deliberate gaps that have to be filled. Crowley's solution was to invoke Mercury daily, a method he taught Frieda Harris to the point where she was channelling Tahuti when painting. We might say that this *Book of Thoth* was written by Tahuti.

Part II and III of 'The Theory of the Tarot' is full of secrets. Comprising not just the Qabalah and Magick with the Tarot, there also are gold nuggets casually scattered, such as references to Kant, and how to discover past lives.

Faced with such riches, there had to be a strategy for writing this book. The primary section is a Commentary on Part I, 'The Theory of the Tarot', including a commentary on *Appendix B*, which concerns the attributions and system of Mercury.

The essays that follow are meditations and studies of topics in *Part I*. The order of these essays are arbitrary so no significance should be attached.

CHAPTER FOUR

The purpose of *The Book of Thoth*

Divination was a daily practice for Aleister Crowley, so naturally he included the system of tarot divination from *Book T* from his slightly modified version published in *The Equinox*. However the clues in *Book T* suggest that this was not the whole system. Crowley recognised this and added several more clues.

The Formula of the Tetragrammaton requires two separate essays which overlap—it is very difficult to unify topics into one chapter. The problem is that many topics can be tackled in different ways.

The *Book of Thoth* is a grimoire inspired by the Society of Eight, loosely disguised as fortune-telling. The *Book of Thoth* was written at the same time as *Book IV* at the height of his powers when Aleister Crowley finally understood the form and function of the TARO. The *Book of Thoth* is understood through initiation, daily invocation, and study of Crowley's writings and historical facts.

Aleister Crowley remained a Christian throughout his life. Shocking as it may seem, this is the conclusion after diligent study of the *Book of Thoth*. To orient the reader, the following points may assist.

- The Abra-melin ritual requires devotion to Christ.
- The Society of Eight: 8 is the number of Christ. 'Society of Eight' is another name of the Jesuits—Kenneth Mackenzie had a sense of humour.
- The purpose of the Society of Eight is to research the Tarot based upon the teachings of Eliphas Levi. As part of that research, the Hermetic Order of the Golden Dawn was proposed, using the Cipher Manuscript and Book T as the basis.
- The SRIA and Quator Coronati are both high grade Masonic groups open only to Master Masons devoted to research.
- Wynn Westcott was member of all three organisations.
- MacGregor Mathers hid the origins of his Golden Dawn with the spurious Frau Sprengel.
- The French influence resurfaces as Martinism, established by Pasqually, who wrote an influential book on the initiated interpretation of the Bible. Adoption of Martinism requires the Mantle and the Mask where the aspirant hides his true character and purpose.
- Society of Eight members John Yarker and Frederick Holland were attempting to establish Martinism in the UK.
- Frederick Holland wrote *Sanctum Sanctorum: The Temple Rebuilt*, and *The Revelation of the Shechinah* which links the Tarot to the Bible, and in particular Revelation.
- Aleister Crowley became friends with John Yarker, who wrote a lengthy review on *Apocalypse Unveiled* (1912) in *The Equinox*.
- The importance of the number 8 is reflected in *The Gospel According to St Bernard Shaw* or *Liber 888* posthumously published in 1953, but Crowley intended it to be published in *The Equinox*, Vol 3, No. 2, according to *The 100th Monkey Press*.
- 888 is the number of Iesous, Jesus. See the writings of James Pryse.

In 1904 Aleister Crowley integrated these concepts in what became *Liber AL*, or the *Book of the Law*. The *Book of the Law* is the term for the Holy Bible as used by Freemasons. 'Thelema' is Will, a Masonic term for Christ. The purpose of *Liber AL* is a ritual performed in the Great Pyramid to break from Mather's Golden Dawn 'abrogate are all rituals', and re-establish the original system found in the Society of Eight. Within *Liber AL* is a verse describing the Ritual of Taphthartharath (a circle with eight candles).

Three years later the A∴A∴ was formed. Much speculation on the meaning of the initials remains inconclusive, but there is a simpler solution—the sum of the two letters and two triangles is 8. The A∴A∴ requires personal study by students, and the curriculum was expanded in *The Equinox* (Libra, balance or Adjustment Atu 8).

Patient study of Crowley's writings on the *Book of Thoth* reveals a pre-occupation of 10, Malkuth, or the Princesses as pendant to the Trinity, or for example the final card, 10 of Disks. This position of the final Heh of YHVH represents energy coming from a strange quarter. Turning to page 10, Crowley juxtaposes the transposition of Tzaddi, while halfway down is a short, rather perplexing section, 'Summary of the Questions Hitherto Discussed'. Here is where Crowley presents exactly the new system, the key to which is found in a crossword puzzle question.

As is often the case, Aleister Crowley never found a worthy successor. Two doughty English women came closest—master magicians Frieda Harris and Dion Fortune, neither of whom entirely succumbed to the blandishments of Thelema.

In summary, the *Book of Thoth* was written to illuminate the teachings and traditions of the Society of Eight, a secret Society of Christian Freemasons. Belief in Christianity is not required in order to enjoy this fascinating book.

The *modus operandi* for continued suppression of Aleister Crowley's message is very simple: decontextualise the book and obsess on the transposition of The Emperor with The Star card as if nothing else is important. Such trivialisation has served its purpose well. The other barrier is to perpetuate the idea that his book was feverishly written while Frieda Harris toiled on the artwork. Knowing that Crowley started the manuscript for *The Book of Thoth* in 1920, facilitates scholarship.

I make no apology for the fragmentary nature of this commentary, for it is part of my own ongoing journey. Aleister Crowley designed the Book of Thoth to be *solve et coagula*. It is up to the reader to integrate the parts into her being. This is process is continuous—there is no final conclusion.

PART TWO

A COMMENTARY ON THE
BOOK OF THOTH

CHAPTER FIVE

Bibliographical note

Grades

Aleister Crowley lists his progress through the Golden Dawn grades from 18 November 1898 up to Portal in November 1899. The footnote continues his progress in January 1900 in Paris after the expulsion. Crowley always considered his magical birthday to be on 18 November.

There is a hiatus until Adeptus Major in April 1904 (after receiving *Liber AL*). The following grades are within the A∴A∴ formed in 1907.

3 December 1910 connected to *Liber 418*. Magus 9° = 2° on 12 October 1915. The grade of Magus is explicitly connected to Atu I throughout the *Book of Thoth*. The letter Beth is Mercury, whose secret attribution is Chokmah (2); the exoteric attribution is the Zodiac which resembles a circle.

Ritual magic in Holborn

While rapidly progressing through the GD grades Crowley was working with George Cecil Jones and Allan Bennett in Holborn where the trio worked on invocation and ritual, particularly of the Goetia.

Meanwhile, Crowley was embarking on the Abra-melin system after purchasing Boleskine in Scotland. As if that was not enough he was working through Masonic grades in Paris!

Working on the Tarot system

Following the grade of Practicus.

> ... he was accordingly entrusted with the secret attributions of the Tarot
> ... He continued these studies alone during his first Voyage the earth in
> search of the Hidden Wisdom.
>
> (Bibliographical Note in the Book of Thoth)

After receiving the Book of the Law (8–10 April 1904) to prepare for the New Aeon ... he published the previously secret attributions of the Tarot in Book 777.

Following Eliphaz Levi, Crowley establishes the universality and inclusiveness of the Tarot.

> much of his magical writing is modelled on, or adorned by references to,
> the Tarot. He published a full account of the Tarot, according to the MSS
> of the Hermetic Order of the Golden Dawn in the Equinox, Vol I, Nos. 7
> and 8 (1912 e.v.).

'The Hermetic Order of the Golden Dawn' is the A∴A∴ formed in 1907.

> During all this time the Tarot was his daily companion, guide, and object
> of research ... He succeeded in uniting under the Schema of the Holy
> Qabalah, of which the Tarot is the greatest single element, all philosophical
> and magical systems soever, including that of the Chinese. This, and his
> 'Naples Arrangement' are with little doubt his greatest achievements
> in scholarship.

Scholarship trumps magical workings and visions in the wider world.

Development of the Tarot deck

> For many years he had deplored the absence of any authentic Text of the
> Tarot. The mediaeval packs are hopelessly corrupt, self-evident, com-
> piled by partisans of existing political systems, or otherwise far from

presenting the Ancient Truth of the Book in a coherent system, or a shape of lucid beauty.

Crowley is referring mainly to French systems and to Mather's Golden Dawn version.

It had from the beginning of his study been his fervent wish to construct a worthy Text.

Secret sources

The beginning was in 1899.

Eliphaz Levi had himself wished to execute a similar task, but succeeded only in leaving us two of the Atu, 'The Chariot' and 'The Devil'.

The Society of Eight was formed by Frederick Holland to develop Eliphaz Levi's system of Tarot, but the members only got as far as these two Atu. It became Crowley's mission to complete their work. The manuscript for the *Book of Thoth* was started in 1920 at the same time as *Book IV*. Then he patiently waited for an artist, which took around 18 years.

Invoking the essential spirit

The Hidden Masters found Frieda Harris to complete the project.

Frieda Harris, who, though she had little or no previous knowledge of the Tarot, possessed in her own right the Essential Spirit of the book.

The final phrase is easily overlooked as hyperbole, but it is a precise description of what happened. Once Frieda Harris had passed her probation, she was initiated into the A∴A∴ and then the real work started; *'possessed in her own right the Essential Spirit of the book'* means Crowley taught Frieda Harris to invoke Mercury twice a day until she was possessed by the spirit. Thoth holds the Double Wand in his right hand (see Frieda Harris' depiction on the back cover).

Together they bent their energies to the formidable task of preparing the 78 cards of the Book of Thoth.

Aleister Crowley, and Frieda Harris inspired by Tahuti,

See the drawing of Thoth on the back cover of the book.

She devoted her genius to the Work.

Tahuti is her "genius".

With incredible rapidity she picked up the rhythm, and with inexhaustible patience submitted to the corrections of the fanatical slave-driver that she had invoked, often painting the same card as many as eight times until it measured up to his Vanadium Steel yardstick!

'Eight times'—the Society of Eight.
'The fanatical slave-driver that she had invoked'—Tahuti. Steel is ruled by Mars. See the *Cephaloedium Working*.

In a short time, Aleister Crowley taught Frieda Harris to invoke Tahuti, or Thoth, into visible appearance. In other words, Frieda Harris became a powerful magician in her own right. While she was wrestling with Tahuti, Crowley was working on the final edit of the book.

Mercury is tricky. For whatever reason Frieda accidentally introduced errors into the invocations, which caused tension between Frieda and Aleister, giving rise to the notion that she had rebelled or somehow manipulated him for her own ends. When he realised what happened, Crowley taught her the Jungitur Mantra.

Jungitur en vati vates; rex inclyte rabdon Hermes tu venias, verba nefanda ferens. Jointly, the bard in the bard, O famous king of the wand, Hermes, mayest thou come bearing unspeakable words.

Invocation for further knowledge

May the passionate 'love under will' which she has stored in this Treasury of Truth and Beauty flow forth from the Splendour and Strength of her work to enlighten the world; may this Tarot serve as a chart for the bold seamen of the New Aeon, to guide them across the Great Sea of Understanding to the City of the Pyramids!

One purpose of this Invocation is to travel from Levi's work *The Book of Splendour* and *Lust* (Atu 11, the number of Magick) to 'enlighten the world'. The Tarot is the map of the New Aeon for traversing Binah to Cairo, City of the Pyramids. 'Splendour and Strength' equally applies to the artwork of the *Book of Thoth*.

Thus, the 'Bibliographical Note' unifies the Tarot with Ritual and Invocation of Tahuti combined with Crowley's research. This was the modus operandi for completing the Tarot started by Eliphaz Levi. Incidentally, the Hebrew letters associated with The Chariot and The Devil are 8 and 70.

Society of Eight and initiation

The Society of Eight was formed to study and develop Eliphaz Levi's system of Tarot. The system required a new order, the Hermetic Order of the Golden Dawn. Mathers stole the system and the name. The only members to escape were W. Wynn Westcott who resigned when he saw Mathers degree-mongering, Allan Bennett who went to Ceylon to study Buddhism, George Cecil Jones and Aleister Crowley reformed the GD as the A∴A∴ in 1907. The common thread to these gentlemen was the magical work performed outside the GD.

Proper understanding of the Tarot involves the wheel of Initiation, Study, Invocation. Initiation is periodical, Study is continuous, Invocation is practised twice daily.

'8 Colour Plates' (unlabelled)

The unnamed '8 Colour Plates' is the biggest clue to the Society of Eight in the *Book of Thoth*. The Atu and Rose Cross in themselves do not suggest any particular insight, but the same plates appear in black and white at the beginning of sections of the book in the same order, pointing to a deeper level of organisation.

Gematria of these plates points to the 'Days of the Week' (page 11), which naturally refers to the number 7, which unites as 78 or the Feminine with the Masculine.

'Eight Plates' is code for *The Magical Ritual of the Sanctum Regnum by Eliphas Levi, 'With Eight Plates'* translated by W. Wynn Westcott, a member of the Society of Eight.

While Crowley may have believed along with the rest of the Golden Dawn membership that Westcott faked the Frau Sprengel letters, at some point he realised the truth that Westcott was innocent, and he used the same device of 8 Plates.

Crowley's emphasis on the complex and ambiguous esoteric relationship between England and Germany continues with the signature at the bottom of the 'Bibliographical Note'.

Martha Küntzel—Soror I.W.E. 8° = 3° A∴A∴

Martha Küntzel (1857–1942) translated Crowley's writings into German, including:

- *Book VI*, Part 1 and 2, 1927
- *Essays on Thelema* 1927
- *The Voice of Silence* 1928
- *The Master Therion's Message* (*Libers 150* and *837*) 1928
- *The Wake World* 1928
- *Science and Buddhism* 1928

Martha Küntzel joined the Theosophical Society in Germany founded by Franz Hartmann and wrote a number of articles on Theosophy.

She also joined the German O.T.O. headed by Theodor Reuss and took the name of Ich Will Es 'I will it'. Crowley met Martha and her partner Otto Gebhardi at the Weida conference in June 1925. What actually happened at Weida is murky to say the least but suffice to say Crowley came out of it very badly. The only good outcome was Martha Küntzel meeting Crowley. Throughout the subsequent backstabbing and plots within the German O.T.O. Martha Küntzel remained loyal to Crowley.

Despite Martha Küntzel's admiration of Adolf Hitler, she was interrogated by the Gestapo over her links to Freemasonry and Aleister Crowley, which naturally changed her ideas. She was lucky, for other O.T.O. members were imprisoned and died in concentration camps for their views.

Uniquely among O.T.O. members, Martha Küntzel enjoyed a consistently warm relationship with Crowley, as seen in their letters where she is always 'little sister'. In contrast Karl Germer constantly brought problems to Crowley. Both Küntzel and Germer were 8° = 3° in the O.T.O.; the fact that Germer is not cited in the *Book of Thoth* strongly suggests that Crowley preferred Martha Küntzel to lead the O.T.O. after the war, but he was not aware of her death in 1942. Possibly Crowley intended to unite the O.T.O. and Theosophy through Martha Küntzel; we will never know.

CHAPTER SIX

The contents of the *Book of Thoth*

Frontispiece

'Wheel and Whoa!' See the *Book of Lies*, Chapter 78. The circularity of the Tarot as the Wheel is emphasised. The extra H has the value of 8 in Coptic, while Heh final represents Malkuth.

Contents, page vii

There are subtle differences between this section and the actual contents of the book. According to the 'Contents', the book is divided into:

Part I: The Theory of the Tarot

    I. Background to the Tarot
    II. Tarot and Qabalistic aspects
    III. Tarot and larger aspects

Part II: The Atu (Keys or Trumps)

    O. The Fool

I to XXI. the other arcana

Presentation of a familiar theme. O is feminine, while I is masculine. Since The Fool is obviously masculine then its feminine attribution gives it hermaphrodite qualities (see Atu VI and XIV). Furthermore, the dualities or permutations of paired Gods associated with The Fool is an expansion of 0 = 2.

Appendix

The citations are divided into three groups.

O. The Fool

I. The Magus

II. Aethyrs from *Liber 418* that describe various Atu.

Part III: The Court Cards

See *Book T* otherwise known as *Liber 78* in *The Equinox*.

Part IV: The Small Cards

'The Four Aces', etc. See *Book T*.

See *Book T* where the order of the cards is in decanate order starting with the 5 of Wands. Crowley uses the sephirotic order of the cards so that it finishes with the 10 of Disks, Wealth. See the *Book of Lies*, Chapter 78:

> *Be this thy task, to see how each card springs necessarily from each other card, even in due order from The Fool unto The Ten of Coins.*

There are two circles, 1 to 36 and Atu 0 to 10 of Disks.

Invocation and Mnemonics

In reality one invocation of Aiwas, 78, the Spirit of the Tarot. The Invocation is the four elements plus Spirit, while the Mnemonics of the Atu are part of a complete system of invocation.

List of illustrations

Text illustrations

Three sets of illustrations

- The Double Loop, The Unicursal Hexagram, Days of the Week
- The Caduceus
- The Essential Dignities of the Planets

Plates

31 Plates; actually 32 if the unnumbered Hierophant is included in the frontispiece. From V to XXIV the plates include four of the cards.

The Text Illustrations represent the Supernal Triangle, while the Plates suggest *Liber AL* as 31 and the 32 rows of the Key Scale.

CHAPTER SEVEN

The Theory of Tarot

The contents of the Tarot

Crowley relates the structure of the Tarot to the Universe and the Holy Qabalah.

The origin of the Tarot

- Egyptian Mysteries
- 14, 15th, or 16th Century
- Geographically, Egypt, the Gypsies, or Indian culture.

Crowley's real view is found in the footnote on page 3 of the *Book of Thoth*:

- ROTA—a wheel
- *Collegium ad Spiritum Sanctum* (a temple)
- *Fama Fraternitatis*—Christian Rosenkreuz

The Wheel contains a complex set of spiritual and magical techniques using gematria, and see the *Book of Lies*, Chapter 78.

For *Collegium ad Spiritum Sanctum* see 'Stepping out of the Old Aeon into the New' by Charles Stansfield Jones (Frater Achad), *The Equinox*, 3.I, which describes a visualisation technique for connecting the student as a point of light in space, i.e. Hadit and Nuit—see *Liber AL*, I.1, and *The Star Sponge Vision*.

The *Fama Fraternitatis* is the primary text of the SRIA headed by Most Worthy Supreme Magus, Dr Wynn Westcott. Only Christians who declare their belief in the Holy Trinity and Christian Rosenkreuz are admitted.

The theory of the correspondences of the Tarot

To the footnote above, modern science, particularly Einstein's Theory of Relativity is added, before returning to gematria—the science of numbers in the Hebrew alphabet. For Crowley's complete essay on numbers see *Liber 58*.

Crowley restates the Tarot as a 'symbolic picture of the Universe, based upon the data of the Holy Qabalah'.

In less than a page, Crowley connects the Tarot to five systems.

Gematria

- 13 is the number of AChD unity and AHBH love. Combined we have 26 YHVH, Unity manifested in Duality.
- 671 is from the Cipher Manuscript, and it is the expansion of ADNY Lord 65. The Lord is Hermes, Thoth, Jesus Christ.
- 671 is ThORA Torah the Law, ThARO Taro, ThROA the Gate (Atu XXI) ROTA, the wheel (Atu X), and AThOR, the goddess Ahathoor.
- 671 is 61 × 11, AIN or Nothing multiplied by the number of Magickal Expansion, from which we derive 0 = 2.

Each number is no more or no less important than any other number—they are all equal in this respect. In Qabalah, numbers represent spiritual beings who belong to a hierarchy. See *The cards of the Tarot as living beings*.

From this we see that the correct spelling of Tarot is Taro. From Levi we understand that the final T tells us that we return to the beginning—another circle.

ADNY is martial energy, which connects to the Magic Square of Mars. Elsewhere Crowley makes the point that Mathers was incorrectly initiated which unbalanced his Mars energy and inflated his ego. Without the influence of Mars, the Solar energy of Tipareth expands exponentially.

The evidence for the initiated tradition of the Tarot

Eliphaz Levi and the Tarot

We return to Eliphas Levi (note the change in spelling). In 1860 Kenneth Mackenzie visits him in Paris to discuss the Tarot, and they agree to collaborate, the consequences of which was the establishment of the secret Society of Eight by Frederick Holland, who knew MacGregor Mathers when they were neighbours near Bournemouth. Holland knew Mathers long before he started using grandiose names, the sign of an unchecked ego.

According to Crowley, Eliphas Levi's view is that 'the Tarot was actually a pictorial form of the Qabalistic Tree of Life'. See 'The Theory of the Correspondences of the Tarot' above.

Dogma and Ritual or Theory and Practice (see 'Bibliographical Note' above) is divided into two sections, both of which have 22 chapters corresponding to the Atu. Crowley would develop the concept into *Liber 231* and in *Book IV*.

However, there is one problem—Eliphas Levi transposed the correspondences in several places.

The Tarot in the Cipher Manuscripts

Having established the true origin of the *Cipher Manuscript*, Crowley delves into the false narrative created by MacGregor Mathers. But first, we return to Freemasonry.

Wynn Westcott was member of Societas Rosicruciana in Anglia (SRIA) and the Quatuor Coronati, both of which only open to Master Masons. MacGregor Mathers was a member of the Quatuor Coronati without distinction; we may suppose this is how the two men met.

As far as the Golden Dawn is concerned Frederick Holland (1854–1917) is air-brushed out; the least I can do is reinstate this remarkable man who established the Society of Eight, and was never a member of the GD.

Born in Birmingham, Frederick Holland moved to Bournemouth, a town mentioned a number of times by Crowley in his writings.

His neighbour was Mathers, and they became friends. Mathers proposed Holland as a Freemason in Lodge of Hengist, No. 195. Holland
was initiated on 3 November 1881, passed on 1 December 1881, and
raised on 5 January 1882, where he remained until March 1887 when he
resigned. Holland co-founded Horsa Lodge, No. 2208 consecrated on
18 December 1887. He resigned this Lodge in September 1890.

Holland joins Lodge of St Cuthberga No. 622 in Wimbourne, Dorset,
on 2 May 1887, the last Craft Lodge he associates with.

For his esoteric studies Holland joins the Metropolitan College of the
SRIA on 13 April 1882 and granted Zelator grade on 20 April 1882, and
the 8th degree on 1 November 1884 with the motto *Vincit qui se vincit*
(he who conquers conquers himself).

Holland taught Mathers alchemy, tarot, and ceremonial work.
Mathers was initially enthusiastic, but the friendship ended some-
time in 1883. See *Sanctum Sanctorum* edited by Darcy Kuntz (2006).
This is one reason why Mathers was never invited to join the Society
of Eight.

The aims of the Society of Eight was the occult study of the Tarot,
alchemy, Hermeticism, and Masonry. However, the membership of
Master Masons was by invitation only and limited to eight. Mathers
proposed Frederick Holland for membership in Freemasonry, but
Holland never returned the favour. That must have rankled Mathers
when he found out. Knowing Mather's flawed Walter Mitty-like character obsessed with status, the principled and Christian Frederick
Holland would never have been part of the GD. Holland's views on the
subject were no doubt similar to Kenneth Mackenzie:

> ... this society means work and not play ... We are practical and not
> visionary, and we are not degree-mongers. That nonsense is played out.
> (Mackenzie to F.G. Irwin, 28 August 1883)

Mathers was all about title and status, taking on the affectation
MacGregor. It could be that it was Holland who informed Westcott of
the liberties Mathers took with his impeccable reputation and slanders,
for in a letter of 31 July 1910, Holland wrote:

> He never mentioned such tosh to me and knew better than to do so for
> I should have laughed him out of court.

The thought occurs that if Holland had been a member, then the Golden Dawn would have been run with discipline and integrity, but that would have meant no scandal, and we would have known as much about the GD as we do with the Society of Eight. Quite possibly Holland's familiarity with the *Cipher Manuscript* would have prevented the whole Sprengel affair from ever happening, and no one would have heard of the Horos couple. Maybe things worked out as they should have done.

Frederick Hockley suffered ill-health and passed in 1885. Subsequently the name of MacGregor Mathers was pencilled in on the membership list. Was this Mathers opportunity for revenge on the sleights he experienced from Frederick Holland? Then there is the religious background. Mathers went all things Celtic and took the members down that route with all the politicking over Ireland and the Celtic Cross spread. Holland would have none of that.

This marks the decline and downfall of the Society of Eight, at least in that form. Other members who survived into the 20th century were John Yarker (see the Ace of Disks) and Wynn Westcott. In Masonic lore, Eight is code for Christ, and the 'Lord'.

Originating from the Society of Eight, once decoded, the *Cipher Manuscript* proposes a new order, the Golden Dawn, a simple set of rituals, and the inclusion of women as members. This is a ground-breaking combination in Masonic circles, where women are still not admitted to this day. Mathers seized the opportunity after Mackenzie died.

Mathers needed unimpeachable witnesses, members of the most august Masonic group, Quator Coronati: Dr Wynn Westcott, Dr Woodford and Dr Woodman to witness the *Cipher Manuscript* and obscure its origins with the Farringdon Road fantasy.

The final paragraph, however, restates the system of the 22 Arcana as originating from Eliphas Levi with the true attributions, and the Society of Eight as 'the promulgators of the Cipher Manuscript, that they were the guardians of a tradition of Truth'.

The Tarot and the Hermetic Order of the Golden Dawn

The title and first paragraph can be equally read as referring to the Society of Eight, or to Mathers version. This is the Trickster Mercury at work.

Crowley alternates paragraphs. The 1st and 3rd refer to his lineage from Levi and the Society of Eight to the A∴A∴, while the 2nd and 4th expand upon the story of the imaginary Frau Sprengel. The footnote refers to Mathers' GD.

The 5th paragraph chronicles Mathers taking over the GD after Westcott had fortuitously resigned and the fact that Mathers never had a connection to the Hidden Chiefs, the evidence of which is that all his knowledge came from the British Library rather than from a higher source. In consequence *'the Order in* its existing form *was destroyed'.*

Paragraph 6 makes an important point, that the serious members were engaged in attempting to get in touch with the Secret Chiefs. One example is the Sphere Group headed by Florence Farr; she eventually confronted Mathers, who astonishingly alleged that it was Westcott who committed the fraud and forged the foundational documents!

Both Westcott and Mathers had the means, the *Cipher Manuscript.* But their motives could not be more opposite. It shows Westcott to be a forward-thinking Mason in allowing women, but such an organisation could only be 'quasi-Masonic'. Westcott was already at the pinnacle of Masonry—he had everything to lose and nothing to gain. Mathers was penniless and ambitious and had everything to gain by any means possible. Both the Society of Eight (means) and the Golden Dawn (motive) were sacrificed by Mathers as his disruptive Mars energy caused chaos.

The importance of contact with the Secret Chiefs cannot be overemphasised. The whole of point of Crowley joining the GD was so that he could meet the Secret Chiefs.

Crowley did not make contact with the Secret Chiefs until 1904; the proof is provided by reception of *Liber AL.* For an account of Crowley's life, *The Confessions, The Equinox of the Gods* and biographical parts of *The Equinox* are highly recommended.

The nature of the evidence

The nature of the evidence is found in the peculiar numbering of the trumps. The counter-change originates in the *Cipher Manuscript* where Strength and Justice are transposed. The purpose of the transposition is to alert the adept to a secret equivalence revealed by Eliphas Levi. The Hebrew letter Shin, value 300, refers to fire, but it is associated with Spirit. The number value of ShYN is 360, the number of degrees of a circle, O; in other words Atu 0 and Atu XX are equivalent. The Hebrew letter Shin and the Hebrew word 'ASh' both mean fire, while The Fool is Spirit. Incidentally this transposition is the reason why the Atu commence with 0. See also *A Vision of Atu 231* below.

Crowley refers to this transposition: 'In the traditional essays and books on the Tarot, the card numbered 'O' was supposed to lie between the cards XX and XXI'.

In order to maintain the secret links to the Society of Eight, Crowley includes the infamous Chapter I, verse 57, which finishes with '*This is also secret; my prophet shall reveal it to the wise*'. If Crowley obeys this injunction, then it is very unlikely that Tzaddi is the Emperor.

'House of God' is one name of Atu XVI, the Tower. Peh, a mouth, completes the letter Aleph, whose first letters form AL, or the *Book of the Law*. However, 'House' is Beth, the second letter of the alphabet corresponding to Mercury or Thoth who communicates by the organ of speech, Peh. Aleph, then, balances the energy of Mars.

> These matters sound rather technical; in fact, they are; but the more one studies the Tarot, the more one perceives the admirable symmetry and perfection of the symbolism. Yet, even to the layman, it ought to be evident that balance and fitness are essential to any perfection, and the elucidation of these two tangles in the last 150 years is undoubtedly a very remarkable phenomenon.

This final paragraph is obscure. The clue is the date reference which hints as Wynn Westcott's translation of *The Magical Ritual of the Sanctum Regnum* by Eliphas Levi (1896):

> The twenty-two Tarot Trumps bear a relation to numbers and to letters; the true attributions are known, so far as it is ascertainable, to but a few students; members of the Hermetic Schools: the attributions given by Levi in his Dogme and Ritual, by Christian, and by Papus are incorrect, presumably by design. The editor has seen a manuscript page of cypher about **150 years** old which has a different attribution, and one which has been found by several occult students, well known to him, to satisfy all the conditions required by occult science.

This editorial is the first public announcement of the existence of the *Cipher Manuscript*. Furthermore, by referencing it confirms that as far as Crowley was concerned, Westcott was innocent of the charges made by Mathers. Why Westcott felt the need to reveal the existence is subject to speculation. Westcott had already left the Golden Dawn, while the Society of Eight had ceased to be a functioning group. Perhaps Wynn Westcott hoped that someone else would take up the reins in the future.

Summary of the questions hitherto discussed

Aleister Crowley designed the *Book of Thoth* as a puzzle to be solved using logic. Logic is pure, mathematical—it does not require religion, dogma, belief, prejudice, or a philosophy. The solution to a puzzle using logic is correct irrespective of how much we agree or disagree with the outcome. Crowley knew this. Crowley includes several mathematical equations in the *Book of Thoth* to illustrate the point.

Gematria is a good example of logic at work. Two or more apparently unconnected ideas or concepts are united when they have the same gematria value. Numbers do not lie, but we trick ourselves as to the meaning of those numbers.

The number 8 is a particularly potent number in the *Book of Thoth*, which is surprising because its significance is not immediately apparent—superficial study of this book is unlikely to trouble the mind of the student with 8, except perhaps as an adjunct to 7. The number 7 is important, but this number will take us in a different direction. Both numbers appear low on the Qabalistic Tree of Life and must be considered as weak. Furthermore, apart from the 8 of Wands, 7 of Wands, and possibly the 8 of Disks, the Minor Arcana associated with these numbers are not appetising; Indolence, Interference, Debauch, Futility, Failure.

Those things that have least value are prized most by alchemists capable of transforming base matter into gold. One of the primary Keys to alchemical work is secrecy and maintaining a contrary outward appearance.

Humility and hiding one's light under a bushel are not qualities associated with Aleister Crowley, but he was particularly adept at concealing his true nature. Maintaining the mask is a highly prized skill in spiritual and magical work.

If you want to understand Aleister Crowley, his *Book of Thoth* is probably the best place to start, even though he carefully hides his personality. The problem is that his disciplines never moved beyond Thelema, even to this day. The *Book of Thoth* addresses this problem.

Understanding this enigmatic work requires a back-to-basics approach and concentration on his writings, preferably the early versions that have not been 'improved' by his followers. Properly understanding the 'clues' in the *Book of Thoth* takes the student on a journey that illuminates obscure areas of his writings bringing interpretations that are very different from the common perception.

For example, Frieda Harris' artwork is critical for the completion of the book for publication, but this was not her greatest achievement while painting the cards.

Taking an honest, open, and unbiased approach will shatter pretty much every preconception. Modern biographies emphasise epochs and name-drop his life: Berlin, India, London, for example; who he met and who he had sex with. While this is all wonderful and entertaining, even titivating in a somewhat prurient way, the problem is that, as Crowley says himself in a number of passages, he was engaged in a secret mission for his entire life commencing with expulsion from the Hermetic Order of the Golden Dawn.

The details of the mission are there for everyone to see—it is hidden in plain sight. Crowley was looking for suitable candidates, but as for the next suitable leader of the O.T.O. none were forthcoming. If anyone took the hints Crowley never said.

The problem is that nobody apart from Crowley ever did the work. Endlessly studying Thelema is an exercise in futility. Worse, embracing Thelema is the trap many fall into. One of his greatest successes was teaching Frieda Harris to be a magician, and she never quite embraced Thelema. She had a healthy disregard for Thelema; she indulged Aleister in it, and she had no aspirations for world domination that blights the occult scene. No doubt Crowley chided and encouraged her, but she held out, only occasionally, and only towards the end of their collaboration did she sign her letters *'Do what thou wilt shall be the whole of the Law'*.

One might ask the question why Crowley put so much effort in to the O.T.O. Master Masons have a responsibility to help brothers irrespective of their Order, and Crowley was a 33° Mason. Without Crowley and John Yarker, the O.T.O. would never have the structure or rituals to function. O.T.O. rituals derive from Freemasonry, some of which had to be changed as they were too similar to the Masons. Crowley was still baby-sitting the O.T.O. on his deathbed when there was in effect only one member.

Crowley tells us what the real work of the TARO involves, 'Invoke often', daily. He even tells us who to invoke and gives the rituals for us to practice, but few magicians ever bother. After all, Thelema is easier, sexier, and promises so much to those who follow their Will. Thelema is the trap that is so easily to fall into, and it is the Key to escape. As Thelemites and other observers have noted, Crowley was a practical joker. Embracing Thelema without daily practice of Invocation only inflames the Ego. Thelema is a test that everyone fails, with the result that we end up with a religion complete with bishops. Thelema is one great practical joke; who likes to admit they were had? Nobody, particularly those with no sense of humour, wants to be made fun of. Freemasons already know the punchline: the *Book of the Law* is the Masonic term for the Holy Bible, while Thelema, 'will', in Masonic terms refers to Jesus Christ.

Nowhere does Crowley require candidates to renounce Christ in order to become a Thelemite, even if some verses in *Liber AL* suggest it.

Threaded throughout the *Book of Thoth* are multi-layered clues that complement and confirm to the Seeker that she is on the right track. Crowley uses a belts and braces approach. As we know, this book is deeply frustrating, compounded by modern false memes designed to take the Seeker further from the source. Put another way, when correctly understood, the *Book of Thoth* shines a light on the life of Aleister Crowley and the correct origins of the Golden Dawn, which is impossible when seen from the perspective of the Golden Dawn.

It is the sense of frustration that engenders the Seeker to entertain heretical thoughts and insights that go entirely against the consensus. Crowley knew the truth was painful, so he added a small section most would ignore:

1. The origin of the Tarot is quite irrelevant, even if it were certain. It must stand or fall as a system on its own merits.
2. It is beyond doubt a deliberate attempt to represent, in pictorial form, the doctrines of the Qabalah.
3. The evidence for this is very much like the evidence brought forward by a person doing a crossword puzzle. He knows from the 'Across' clues that his word is 'SCRUN blank H'; so it is certain, beyond error, that the blank must be a 'C'.
4. These attributions are in one sense a conventional, symbolic map; such could be invented by some person or persons of great artistic imagination and ingenuity combined with almost unthinkably great scholarship and philosophical clarity.
5. Such persons, however eminent we may suppose them to have been, are not quite capable of making a system so abstruse in its entirety

without the assistance of superiors whose mental processes were) or are, pertaining to a higher Dimension.

This section on page 10 of the *Book of Thoth* is easily overlooked, particularly as it faces three 'Text Illustrations' that are much more interesting: the unicursal Hexagram, the 'Days of the Week', and 'proof' of the transposition of Tzaddi with Heh.

The secrets Crowley hid all his life are not going to be easily revealed. Crowley knew that without help from him, the *Book of Thoth* would forever remain inscrutable. The incongruity of scrunch as the answer to a crossword clue and the logical certainty of the missing c is a lifeline to a desperate researcher who is making minimal gains.

Qabalistic analysis of scrunch does give some insight, but since neither the needle nor the haystack have been located, assistance is limited. Not knowing what to look for hobbles research. This was my experience. It was not until I had assembled the facts and came to the right conclusions that I found myself circling back to scrunch. Now I knew what to look for, I marvelled at Crowley's genius in hiding the solution in plain sight.

Unless one is prepared to abandon all preconceptions about Aleister Crowley, his life, and his philosophy, *scrunch* will for ever be an absurd *non sequitor*. One of the shocks is the realisation that Crowley uncovered the truth about 8 in around 1900, his lifetime work was to secretly perpetuate the knowledge of 8 in his own Order so that it would not be lost. Unfortunately, he buried the secret so well, that it was in danger of never being found. Hence the need for the *Book of Thoth*. The funny thing is that once the importance of 8 is realised, references to it are obvious in Crowley's writings. Furthermore, this number is key to understanding other cryptic systems in his writings, including *Liber AL*.

My first inkling of the importance of this number was when I took notice of the colour plates in the *Book of Thoth*, an extravagance in the paper shortages of war-torn England of 1944. With '8 Colour Plates', whose gematria takes us to the 'Days of the Week' on page 11. Crowley was not the first to use 8 Colour Plates as a code—that honour belongs to his previous incarnation as Eliphas Levi. Even so, 8 becomes an obsession, an obsession for magicians and mystics alike down the centuries.

Now that the secret has been revealed, we return to page 10.

1. The origin of the Tarot is quite irrelevant, even if it were certain.

Classic Crowley. Of course, the origin of the Tarot is important, but which origin? Crowley dismisses the classical and mediaeval theories in a short paragraph. He is obviously thinking of other origins.

It must stand or fall as a system on its own merits

Here is the criteria. The system has to be tested, which is not something we associate with the Tarot. Crowley is inviting the reader to test his system, and as we know from an initial reading, the *Book of Thoth* does not make sense, therefore the 'system' fails. There are many hypothesises and systems to test, and unless you are very lucky, all will fail.

The scientific process: hypothesise, test, analyse, re-hypothesise, and so on. Once a system has been established, it has to be tested in the wild. One of the tests is 'does this hypothesis add, illuminate, or give insights to Crowley's voluminous writings?' Even when on the right track, insights will not make sense until more corroborating evidence is found.

In other words, Crowley is inviting the Seeker to test not just the *Book of Thoth*, but test it against his entire philosophical, magical and mystical writings! Such an undertaking is life-changing for the Seeker. Put another way, Crowley opens a window to his mind through the agency of the Tarot.

2. It is beyond doubt a deliberate attempt to represent, in pictorial form, the doctrines of the Qabalah

The doctrines of Qabalah in pictorial form is a very common view. Superficially, Crowley is inviting the Seeker to test the validity or veracity of that doctrine. Deconstructing the sentence takes us to a different view: 'beyond doubt' a 'deliberate attempt to represent', the certainty is the deliberate attempt to represent this doctrine. Other words, this doctrine is false. The Seeker has to find another way.

3. The evidence for this is very much like the evidence brought forward by a person doing a crossword puzzle. He knows from the 'Across' clues that his word is 'SCRUN blank H'; so it is certain, beyond error, that the blank must be a 'C'.

'The evidence for this' refers not to the Qabalistic argument, but to the secret system hidden within the *Book of Thoth*.

Crowley is telling us to look for the blanks in the text and then find clues that enable those blanks to be filled. If the logic is correct, then there is no error.

With hindsight, it is obvious that Crowley is talking about himself setting the puzzle, and he even tells us that the answer will be: 'a crossword' and 'Across'. The blank must be a 'C' is another clue that makes no sense at the beginning of the journey, but when the journey is complete the Seeker will realise that C is the surname of two mythical people found in the footnote on page 3.

Note the repetition of 'blank'. Blank is a space or Zero, while H could refer to the Emperor, but Crowley sees H as a Greek letter, which has the value of 8. Take the first and last letters of scrunch and we have Shin 300 and 360, Atu 20. Take the same two letters using the Greek value we have S8, initials of a mysterious Masonic group. Cheth is the 8th letter whose analysis is 418, and it is the first letter of the second sephirah Chokmah; 8 is the number of Mercury, who is attributed to Thoth and Hermes and other Mercurial gods. Masons will note that 8 is the number of Christ. Is there other evidence of the importance of 8 in this analysis? RUN is 256, a power of eight.

Scrunch is an onomatopoeic word; sound relates to Spirit. To scrunch is to crumple or crush something, here, it has the sense of unifying. Scrunch has seven letters, with a blank it is reduced to 6, which is Solar, and the sephirah of Christ and Christian Rosenkreuz, while if we include the second C with the blank we have eight letters.

There are other Qabalistic games we can play. Scrunch includes CRC, the initials of Christian Rosenkreuz, while Resh is Solar, Atu XIX. N is Atu XIII, Death means Initiation, and refers to the resurrection of Christ and the Tomb of Christian Rosenkreuz. Vau is 6, another Solar reference.

SCRUNCH = 361 or 364 depending on the value of H, if we add the Zero, we come to 365, which might be stretching a point. Either way, the number of SCRUNCH falls between 360 the circle, and 365 the days of the year. See page 27. Both numbers indicate a circle. Crowley says about 361:

ADNI HARTz, the Lord of the Earth. Note 361 denotes the 3 Supernals, the 6 members of Ruach, and Malkuth. This name of God therefore embraces all the 10 Sephiroth.

SCRUN-H is 341, the sum of the Mother Letters; see *Liber HHH.*

Hidden within SCRUNCH is the Goddess Nu, 56 a number critical to analysis of *Liber AL*, I.1, and, of course, it is the total of the Court Cards and Minor Arcana. Subtract 56 from 78 (note the sequence) and we have 22, the number of Atu; 78 is another number that pertains to *Liber AL*.

- 256, a number of Mercury yields URN, see *Liber 73*
- SC = 80 plus 256 and 8 is 344, *PRDS Paradise*
- CR = 220 verses of *Liber AL*
- RU = 206
- NC = 70
- NH = 55 or 58
- NCH = 75 or 78
- SR = 260 a Mercurial number
- SV = 66
- SH = 65

Roman numbers on the Atu

20 + 10 + 19 + 5 + 13 + 20 + 5 = 92
20 + 10 + 19 + 5 + 13 + 20 + 7 = 94
20 + 10 + 19 + 5 + 13 + 5 = 72
20 + 10 + 19 + 5 + 13 + 7 = 74

CHR = KHR, the 20th Aire, is an anagram of RHK, Ra-Hoor-Khuit. RHK is 225 or 228, but in the 20th Aethyr the value is 308. This confirms the link to Liber 418.

The two crosses (a cross and a crossword) both symbolise 4; added together they are either 8 or 44, the number of DM, blood. See the *Book of Lies*, Chapter 44.

In a roundabout way, this analysis of unpromising material, a word offered by Crowley that on the face of it has nothing to do with the matter, confirms point 2 above, so he was right about it after all.

Armed with the facts, the Seeker then needs to verify the system. The question to ask is 'where did he get this from?'. Crowley anticipates this:

4. These attributions are in one sense a conventional, symbolic map; such could be invented by some person or persons of great artistic imagination and ingenuity combined with almost unthinkably great scholarship and philosophical clarity.

- *'These attributions'* refer to the analysis of SCRUNCH.
- *'a conventional, symbolic map'*. This system is not new. In other words, Crowley did not invent it. The system applies to the conventional maps we already have.
- *'person or persons'* unnamed or unknown, but quite possibly refer to members mentioned in the footnote on page 3.
- *'great artistic imagination and ingenuity combined with almost unthinkably great scholarship and philosophical clarity'*. Crowley is not one to heap praise.
- One unknown philosopher is Louis Claude de Saint-Martin, founder of Martinism.
- Unquestionably, the second half of the 19th century bursts at the seams with talented magicians, most of whom are unknown to tarot students.

5. Such persons, however eminent we may suppose them to have been, are not quite capable of making a system so abstruse in its entirety without the assistance of superiors whose mental processes were) or are, pertaining to a higher Dimension.

'... a system ... without the assistance of superiors ... mental processes ... a higher Dimension'. Aleister Crowley was guided by the Secret Chiefs or Hidden Masters.

Now that the bare bones of the system are in place, we have to re-construct the skeleton and add flesh.

In point 1 Crowley states that the system has to stand or fall on its own merits. In the preceding chapters he presents the system as used by the Hermetic Order of the Golden Dawn, which failed because its founder, MacGregor Mathers, never had contact with the Hidden Masters. Mathers and Crowley had exactly the same influences— modern-day Cain and Abel.

Masonic Key to 8

This same history of the Golden Dawn gives clues as to the significance of 8 via Freemasonry.

On page 5, Crowley makes clear 'The Evidence for the Initiated Tradition of the Tarot' resides with Eliphaz Levi and Kenneth Mackenzie. In 1850 Mackenzie spent a weekend in Paris with Levi, where they discussed the Tarot in-depth and agreed to work on a new Tarot scientifically designed. Since both were magicians, this deck is magical. The ambition was never fulfilled due to Levi's death in 1875.

However, *Dogma and Ritual* by Levi is the template for *Book IV*, while his designs for The Chariot and for The Devil are depicted in the *Book of Thoth*. The letters associated with these two cards are Cheth and AIN, 8 and 70, respectively.

In the final paragraph Crowley mentions the 'Order of Initiates' who appear in the next section, 'The Tarot in the Cipher Manuscripts'. Being a Mason, Crowley is very respectful to Masonic groups. On page 3 he mentions the SRIA, a Christian Master Mason Society, dedicated to the *Fama Fraternitatis*, while here on page 6 we are introduced to the Quatuor Coronati Lodge of Freemasonry, another group of Master Masons dedicated to research. Neither group is interested in degrees, for their members have already reached high status. Crowley was never a member of either organisations, reasons for which will be discussed later.

Dr Wynn Westcott, Dr Woodford, and Dr Woodman, so the story goes, discovered loose papers in a Farringdon Road bookshop. These papers were destined to be the basis of the Hermetic Order of the Golden Dawn. The origin of these papers is mysterious, but Crowley has no doubt that Levi is the author, for the transposition of the Atu mentioned on page 5 is repeated on page 6. This bunch of papers is now known as the *Cipher Manuscript*.

Having established the true attributions of the Tarot, Crowley acknowledges the promulgators of the *Cipher Manuscript* as guardians of a 'Tradition of Truth' i.e. ToT or Thoth.

Moving on to the third section 'The Tarot and the Hermetic Order of the Golden Dawn'. Crowley does something very clever with the first paragraph which is presented as a statement of truth:

> *One must now digress into the history of the Hermetic Order of the Golden Dawn, the society reconstituted by Dr. Westcott and his colleagues, in order to show further evidence as to the authenticity of the claim of the promulgators of the Cipher Manuscript.*

The reader naturally assumes Crowley is talking about what follows, an account of how Samuel Liddell Mathers formed the Golden Dawn. However, this can equally apply to Crowley's own Hermetic Order of the Golden Dawn established upon the authority of the secret Society formed by Kenneth Mackenzie, which includes Eliphaz Levi and Wynn Westcott for the purpose of esoteric research particularly into the Tarot. In other words, the Society of Eight was formed of Master Masons to develop the Tarot of Eliphaz Levi. The two primary documents for this were the *Cipher Manuscript* and *Book T*.

Digression complete, we return to the narrative which interlaces Crowley's secret Golden Dawn with Mathers' version. What follows is controversial on so many levels, for where the truth lies depends on one's views of MacGregor Mathers as much as on Aleister Crowley.

As the senior Mason, Dr Westcott is tasked with contacting Fräulein Sprengel whose name and address appears on a page of the *Cipher Manuscript*. Fräulein Sprengel is a representative of the Hidden Masters. This is a big deal. Crowley joined the GD solely so that he could meet the Hidden Masters or Secret Chiefs. Nobody knew who the Secret Chiefs were, but now there was an address of one in Germany.

The significance of the German connection requires another digression. Germany was the mythic home of Christian Rosenkreuz, and the primary focus of the SRIA. The Society of Eight determined the right of women to join Freemasonry, but which still today does not admit women. With this progressive nature, it is perhaps not surprising that Fr Sprengel appears. As we know, Fr Sprengel is as elusive as the Hidden Masters. In adding an extra page to the document, Mathers ticks all the right boxes. Despite 'almost' joining the Society of Eight, Mathers had no status, but Dr Westcott had the perfect Masonic pedigree. Westcott was independently wealthy and had no interest in recruitment while the permanently penniless Mathers was desperate to enhance his status and make money. Even though a member of the Society of Eight, Westcott probably had little interest in the *Cipher Manuscript* with its focus on ritual—when Mathers shows him the document complete with contact page, he is naturally impressed that the Society of Eight had contact with the Rosicrucians in Germany. In other words, Westcott was Mathers' patsy right from the start.

Page 11—three diagrams

The Unicursal Hexagram

The Unicursal Hexagram is drawn without the pen lifting off the paper. At the centre is a five petalled rose, indicating the 5° = 6° grades and the Rosy Cross; 6 refers to the altar, while there are five tattwas.

The days of the week

Crowley deliberately misidentifies the Heptagon and Heptagram as Hexagon and Hexagram and to compound the error he mischievously ascribes it all to MacGregor Mathers! The days of the week are generated from the planetary hours which are important when performing ritual work. Mercury takes on the energy of the sign and other planets aspecting it. The seven planets correspond to the seven-lettered name Babalon, or Venus.

The double loop in the Zodiac

Technically there are three loops which are equivalent to three zeros. At the centre is the vesica piscis formed by intersecting circles. The vesica piscis is the basis of the temple, and the female organ. Here we square the circle. See *A Vision of Atu 231.*

CHAPTER EIGHT

The Tarot and the Holy Qabalah

C rowley returns to the numbers 1 to 10, basis of the Minor Arcana and the Sephiroth on the Qabalistic Tree of Life, starting with zero which can mean anything you want rather than nothing. The following chapters present a logical progression useful in magical and spiritual work.

'The Naples Arrangement'

So called because it was formulated in Naples. However, the development of these ideas can be found in various Masonic teachings. There is a deviation for the numbers 7, 8, and 9 which correspond to Sat, Chit, and Ananda; this is clearly from another teaching which we will come back to later.

The Book of the Great Auk

Because numbers are positions, it is possible to go backwards through to the origin, in other words a method of knowing previous incarnations. The primary position for this is at 7, 8, and 9, or Being, Thought, and Bliss. Building from 0 we go to 10, which has a zero. Another method is to use the 40 Minor Arcana.

The Tarot and the Formula of Tetragrammaton

Negative numbers are now introduced, which is another way of describing zero: −1 + 1 = 0 a retrogression. Better if they are translated into active and passive or male and female to create a Son and a Daughter; now there are four distinct substances which in alchemical terms become the four elements.

Exactly what these elements represent at any one moment is a problem of perspective—we all have a unique point of view.

In terms of knowns and unknowns, the Son is a Known Known, while the Daughter is an Unknown Known, a doctrine of which becomes more pertinent when it comes to Atu 0.

The Tarot and the elements

The three known elements in the previous chapter become Fire, Water, and Air, or the Three Gunas, which have the qualities of Sulphur, Mercury, and Salt. Sulphur is activity, energy is desire, while Mercury is Fluidity, Intelligence, the power of Transmission. Salt is inert unless it reacts upon the activities of Sulphur and Mercury. Fire, Water, and Air are the Three Mother Letters, spiritual energy that manifests in the fourth element Earth, which is Tau, the last letter, or the Daughter, pendant to 7, 8, and 9 as 10. YHVH is representative of this dynamic process.

Crowley works through the titles and names of the Court Cards familiar to tarot students, but then he expands the system as it returns to zero. He is describing the model used in the Golden Dawn teaching on the tarot as it pertains to the Qabalistic Tree of Life (The Concourse of the Forces), which is limited.

The alternative is to place the Father, Mother, Son and Daughter on the rim of the wheel where they move about on the motionless axis of Zero, which has no beginning or end.

Finally, he names the four elements as Wands, Cups, Swords, and Disks.

Crowley analyses 4 in other ways, starting with YHVH, four levels on the Qabalistic Tree of Life as parts of the soul, the four worlds, which are confusing and require greater study. Once that greater understanding has been achieved, it is time to look at the relations between the numbers known as Paths or Netibuth, which are 22 in number and correspond, of course, with the Atu.

Kantian Sense

Now the Sephiroth, which are emanations of the number 1, as already shown, are things-in-themselves, in almost the Kantian sense. The lines joining them are Forces of Nature, of a much less complete type; they are less abstruse, less abstract.

Immanuel Kant (1724–1804) synthesised early modern rationalism and empiricism. Allan Bennett possibly introduced Kant to Crowley in the late 1890s—see *Science and Buddhism* (1903). Crowley uses Kant's methodology as a means for understanding Kabbalism. The Sephiroth are *things-in-themselves* (plural of *ding an sich*), therefore unknowns (*noumenon*). However, the lines connecting the Sephiroth, i.e. the 22 Hebrew letters or Atu are not so unknown (*phenomenon*). See page 4 for Crowley's insights into a number as a thing-in-itself.

A thing can be a point, a thought, spirit, a person, or a star, anything. '*Every man and every woman is a star*' is a good example. Space is the distance between two things, which is much more helpful than seeing nebulous space as Akasha. *The Star Sponge Vision* reflects Kantian qualities. Thoughts are sequential things, so follow them back to the source and you have the basis for discovering past lives, which concerns the *Book of the Great Auk*.

The two versions of the 'Naples Arrangement' are Crowley's interpretations of Kant's 'Transcendental Reality' in space. Key to the system is the synthetic *a priori* proposition where an object contains information that is not present in the subject, but the truth value of the proposition can be obtained without recourse to experience. An example often cited is that '*a triangle's interior angles are equal to 180°*'. Crowley expands on this statement which is not true for a triangle on a curved surface—Riemann's non-Euclidean geometry and Einstein's curvature of space and time.

Given Crowley's notoriety, his espousal of Kant may come as a surprise, but Kant's extreme ethical theory balances Thelemic ideas. The 'categorical imperative' states that one should always respect the humanity in others, and that one should only act in accordance with rules that hold for everyone.

The 22 Keys, Atu, or trumps of the tarot

Despite the title, Crowley includes sections on the Minor Arcana and the Court Cards as a means of unification. Working through this chapter is something of a slog, but persevere because there is treasure.

Major Arcana

Aleister commences this chapter with a reminder to use all 78 cards otherwise there will be imbalance, particularly when the Atu are used as magical formulae (see *Book IV*). The point is that we are not talking about mere cards, but representations of the entire Universe. The primary attribution is through the Hebrew alphabet and the *Sepher Yetsirah*.

Continued work with these Atu brings awareness of their personality (i.e. as spirits), the building blocks for the Temple.

Aleister has some interesting insights on the Atu.

> *They are rather hieroglyphs of peculiar mysteries connected with each. One may begin to suspect that the Tarot is not a mere straightforward representation of the Universe in the impersonal way of the system of the Yi King. The Tarot is beginning to look like Propaganda. It is as if the Secret Chiefs of the Great Order, which is the guardian of the destinies of the human race, had wished to put forward certain particular aspects of the Universe; to establish certain especial doctrines; to declare certain modes of working, proper to the existing political situations. They differ; somewhat as a literary composition differs from a dictionary.*

Path working

> *The Tarot trumps are twenty-two in number; they represent the elements between the Sephiroth or things-in-themselves, so that their position on the Tree of Life is significant. Here are one or two examples.*

'Children of the Voice, the Oracle of the Mighty Gods' is a secret title from *Book T*, and Crowley suggests the derivation, for this path is from Tiphareth to Binah, 6 to 3.

The second example is the High Priestess or 'Heavenly Isis' from 6 to 1:

> *The card represents the Heavenly Isis. It is a symbol of complete spiritual purity; it is initiation in its most secret and intimate form, descending upon the human consciousness from the ultimate divine consciousness. Looked at from below, it is the pure and unwavering aspiration of the man to the Godhead, his source.*

Crowley then makes a very interesting observation:

> *From the foregoing it will be clear that the Tarot illustrates, first of all, the Tree of Life in its universal aspect, and secondly, the particular comment illustrating that phase of the Tree of Life which is of peculiar interest to those persons charged with the guardianship of the human race at the particular moment of the production of any given authorised pack.*

The *'particular comment'* refers to the title of the card, a preamble for introducing the change of status to the Aeon on 21 March 1904.

The double-wanded one

The *'double-wanded one'* is *'Thmaist of dual form as Thmais and Thmait'*, from whom the Greeks derived their Themis, goddess of Justice. Thmaist is the Hegemon, who bears a mitre-headed sceptre, like that of Joshua in the Royal Arch Degree of Freemasonry. He is the third officer in rank in the Neophyte Ritual of the G∴D∴, following Horus as Horus follows Osiris. He can then assume the 'throne and place' of the Ruler of the Temple when the 'Equinox of Horus' comes to an end.

> It has consequently been the endeavour of the present scribe to preserve those essential features of the Tarot which are independent of the periodic changes of Aeon, while bringing up to date those dogmatic and artistic features of the Tarot which have become unintelligible. The art of progress is to keep intact the Eternal; yet to adopt an advance-guard, perhaps in some cases almost revolutionary, position in respect of such accidents as are subject to the empire of Time.

While artistic styles change, the underlying message stays the same.

The order of things

Related to Kant's 'thing-in-itself' is the order of things, which have various categories and appear in Masonic and Crowley's writings.

- Divine Order
- Intelligible Order
- Established Order or Accepted Order
- True Order
- Natural Order

Some of these orders relate to orders of spirits. See Kant, *Dreams of a Spirit-Seer*.

CHAPTER NINE

The Tarot and the Universe

I n Part II, the Tarot was defined vertically on the Qabalistic Tree of Life. In Part III the definition is circular.
Once again Crowley repeats a favourite definition;

> The TAROT is a Pictorial representation of the Forces of Nature as conceived by the Ancients according to a conventional symbolism.

In his short introduction the nature of the Zodiac is compared to the Wheel, ROTA, which is a poetic way of attributing Chokmah, the second sephira, to Mercury.

Theories of the ancients

1. Where is the centre?

In infinite space, the centre is always an arbitrary point—we need flexibility in our thinking.

2. The Solar System

The Zodiac has 12 divisions, starting with four divisions—the four elements (but not as we think).

The four elements are multiplied by three.

For the Sun, time is measured by change of the length of the day. On the Equinox the length of the day = length of the night. On one side we see Aries, on the other side we see Libra.

For the Moon time is measured from Full Moon to Full Moon, approximately 28 days as 28 Mansions.

360 days in a year.

The divine name Mithras adds up to 360 so the spelling was changed to Meithras 365, the same as Abraxas. See Crowley's commentary on *AL* I.1 for a full explanation.

360 divided by 10 gives us the 36 decanates corresponding to the Minor Arcana excluding the Aces. Quartering the circle gives us the square.

4. Subdivision of the elements in the Zodiac

The qualities of the elements is defined as Cardinal, Fixed, and Mutable in the Zodiac, but we take into account the planetary influences. See page 286.

5. Extending the subdivisions

The Dyad or Two is key to understanding subdivisions, for there are only two operations: to divide and to unite, or the alchemical *solve et coagula*.

Classification is the method for grouping objects of a similar quality—apples and pears.

Arising from this Crowley returns to 0 = 2 as 1 + –1, which allows him to introduce Chinese cosmology as Yang and Yin, in other words that most Mercurial system of the *I Ching*.

6. Unifying the Tree of Life with the I Ching

The sum of the Sephiroth and the 22 Paths is 32, which is half the number of hexagrams, 64. See *Liber 777*.

The Tree of Life

1. Perspective A is not perspective B

However we view the Tarot, it is still the same for all. The Tarot is not dead—it is alive, dynamic.

2. Numbers as the basis of reality

Numbers have symbolic qualities. The thing-in-itself of 4 symbolises Law, Restraint, Power, Protection, and Stability.

- Zero in three forms
- Tao manifests through Teh
- Shiva manifests through Shakti

The 'Naples Arrangement'

The ten things-in-themselves defined from the point. Note another system from Points 7 to 9 converging to 10.

Paragraph 4 restates Atu II and Atu VI in terms of their Paths from 1 to 6 and 3 to 6 respectively.

The final sentence *'The individual Fixed Stars do not enter into the system of the Tarot'* is curious, for when Crowley uses negation in a statement the opposite is often true. Mathers' system incorrectly attributes the Minor Arcana to constellations in the Southern Hemisphere.

The Tarot and the Tree of Life

Time for another definition of the Tarot:

> The Book of Thoth or Tahuti—is the influence of the Ten Numbers and the Twenty-two Letters on man, and his best methods of manipulating their forces.

Clearly the best method is via the Wands, for the rest of this chapter is devoted to an analysis of these 14 cards including natural phenomena (the Triplicities): 10 × 22 = 220, the number of verses in *Liber AL*.

The Atu of Tahuti

'Atu' is House or Key. House in Hebrew is Beth, identical to the second letter of the Hebrew alphabet ruled by Mercury, which makes Atu of Tahuti equivalent to 'Mercury of Mercury' or Mercury squared. 'Key' reminds us of *The Key of the Mysteries* by Eliphas Levi. Mercury in the Key Scale is 12, squared is 144.

> Section IV
> *144, A square and therefore a materialisation of the number 12. Hence the numbers in the Apocalypse. 144,000 only means 12 (the perfect number in the Zodiac or houses of heaven and tribes of Israel) x 12, i.e. settled x 1000, i.e. on the grand scale.*
>
> (*Liber 58*)

The *Apocalypse* is emphasised for the Kingdom of Heaven.
The Twenty-two Houses of Wisdom has three definitions:

• We have already established that the secret ruler of Chokmah, Wisdom is Mercury.
• The 22 trumps of the Tarot.
• The letter of the Hebrew alphabet corresponding to the Paths.

We return to the *Sepher Yetsirah* concerning Mother Letters, Single Letters, and Double Letters. The problem is that there are four elements not three, while Spirit is missing, which Crowley discussed previously, but now he unifies the system with the *Pentagram of Salvation* YHShVH, in other words, Jesus.

Tahuti is the Lord of Wisdom, a venerable title used when invoking him. The Keys are guides to conduct, the map of the Kingdom of Heaven, the best way to take it by force (see Wands previously). Understanding of the magical problem is necessary for successful invocation, which is always an inner process.

The rest of the chapter is an expansion of the idea of study in terms of 'Tactics and Strategy':

> The student of the Tarot must not therefore expect to find anything beyond a careful selection of the facts about any given card, a selection made for a quite definite magical purpose.

See page 265.

The Roman numbers of the trumps

This section is very similar to 'The Nature of the Evidence', page 8. Crowley draws our attention to it in the footnote so we know it is not a mistake. See *A Vision of Atu 231*.

The Tarot and magick

Crowley defines magick as *'the science and art of causing change to occur in the conformity with the Will'* but we have been discussing invocation in the previous sections:

• The Tarot and the Tree of Life: manipulating forces (Wands)
• The Atu of Tahuti: Invocation of Mercury
• The Roman Numbers of the Trumps: the New Aeon

Re-ordering these points, Invocation of Mercury uses the Powers and Space (i.e. Points) and Time (Future).

The commentary in this section appears to be a reversion to the old system until we get to page 43 when the 5 of Wands is analysed in detail. This card marks the commencement of the year in Leo, not in Aries (2 of Wands). The importance of which is to communicate with the Intelligences of the cards and introduce the Goetia and the 'Great Name of God'.

The Shemhamphorasch and the Tarot

Deriving the 72 names from Exodus XIV verses 19, 20, and 21 is entirely traditional, to which we add the powers of:

• Quinaries
• Angels
• Demons
• Magical images
• Lord of Triplicities
• Lesser Assistant Angels etc
• Corresponding demons

The Tarot and ceremonial magick

Thus far Crowley has preferred invocation as aspiration to the highest, but there is also evocation, favoured by most magicians. Evocation does not require sympathy—hostility is favoured at some level.

The Tarot and animism

Types of superstition which often result in fear. 'The Sacred Magic of Abra-melin' is a good example, but Crowley was using this system while still working through the grades of Mather's Golden Dawn. The Abra-melin spirits seek out the Magician.

The cards of the Tarot as living beings

Crowley's view of invocation and evocation expanded:

> The adepts of the Tarot would say, quite simply, 'We are alive and the planet is alive, so we can make friends. If you kill the plant first, you are asking for trouble'.

Finally,

> Each card is, in a sense, a living being; and its relations with its neighbours are what one might call diplomatic. It is for the student to build these living stones into his living Temple.

As established previously, the Temple is Beth in Hebrew, the letter ruled by Mercury. 'Living Stones' see The Temple of Solomon serialised in The Equinox.

Invocation

The Invocation appears at the junction point between Venus and Mercury. Venus rules the tarot cards while Mercury rules invocation.

In the invocation Aiwaz rules the five elements, while his number is 78—he is a unitary force. Placed between the 7 and 8 we get 718, the number of Perdurabo, 'Abomination of Desolation' and the Stele of Revealing.

The 'Dawn Meditation' was regularly practised by Aleister Crowley.

Plates

Black and white prints of all 78 cards, four to a plate, commencing with The Fool and ending with the 10 of Disks.

This marks the completion of the first part of the book corresponding to Babalon and Venus. The second part is ruled by Mercury which covers divination, invocation, and initiation.

CHAPTER TEN

Appendix A of the *Book of Thoth*

The behaviour of the tarot: Its use in the art of divination

See 'The Cards of the Tarot as Living Beings'.

Crowley emphasises the importance of familiarity with the cards which comes from prolonged contact. In short we have to live with the cards, and they have to live with us.

> *The ideal way is that of contemplation. But this involves initiation of such high degree that it is impossible to describe the method in this place.*

Crowley hints at the method taught to Frieda Harris in the 'Bibliographical Note'. The method of divination is found in *Book T*.

Practical experience of reading the tarot professionally shows that the First Operation is efficacious for most questions. See my 'The Tarot and the Magus' and 'Beyond the Celtic Cross' for more details.

However, there is a problem with the system—it is impossible to cut the cards into equal stacks. The glaring omission from the system is that of the planets. Seven stacks of 11 cards with a Significator is the obvious solution—see the ABRAHADABRA spread below; 77 is the number of OZ, Strength. See Chapter 77 of the *Book of Lies*.

This very powerful system of the seven planets spread complements the invocation of the 8, and guards against the abuse of divination warned by Crowley at the end of this section.

The Amalantrah Working, *Liber 729*, gives many examples of divination uniting gematria, the Tarot and the *I Ching*.

General characters of the trumps as they appear in use

The divinatory meanings are derived from *Book T*.

CHAPTER ELEVEN

Appendix B of the *Book of Thoth*

Correspondences

Continuing the theme of living beings and their relations, Crowley expands the notion. The units are natural numbers and mathematical terms.

The number 93 enumerates to Thelema in Greek, while 31 is AL; 13 is AChD. See the footnote to The Juggler.

Crowley then lists the correspondences of Mercury. The choice of this planet is no accident.

At this point the tables of the Four Scales of Colour are mentioned. Occult colour theory ultimately derives from Masonic sources and is a system of magick in its own right. See *777* page 67 for Crowley's commentary on the colours.

Diagram 1. The Key Scale [Or: The Tree of Life, with the attribution of the Sephiroth and the Paths]

Back to basics. These attributions need to be memorised, so they become instinctual.

Diagram 2. The general attributions of the tarot
[Or: The Tarot on the Tree of Life]

The Tree in terms of YHVH and the Court Cards.

Diagram 3. The Chinese cosmos [Or: The Yi King on the Tree of Life]

The *I Ching* is a Mercurial system. Crowley wrote a book on the subject, where he renamed two of the trigrams as Lingam and Yoni. See 'Wheel and Whoa!'

Diagram 4. The Caduceus of Hermes

The Caduceus is the primary symbol of Mercury or Thoth uniting the Sephiroth with the Mother Letters.

> ... it is necessary to learn how to transmute instinctively and automati-
> cally every simple symbol into every complex symbol and back again, for
> it is possible to realise the unity and diversity which is the solution of the
> cosmic problems.

Another example of *solve et coagula*.

Diagram 5. The numbers of the planets

See the diagram of the Hexagram opposite this page and the Unicursal Hexagram on page 11. The numbers on this diagram are traditional and derive from the corresponding magic squares. As a bonus he is referring to the 'Days of the Week' on the same page, which is misattributed to the Hexagon and the Hexagram.

However, the text only makes sense if one studies the Sephiroth on Tree of Life with the planetary correspondences.

Crowley then introduces Malkuth which refers to Earth and to the Heh final or Daughter as a way of discussing Christianity and Freemasonry in the same breath. In fact, he is discussing Diagram 4.

Diagram 6, 7, and 8

The three pentagrams shown on page 275:

• The Elements and their symbols

- The Elemental Weapons
- The Sphinx

Diagram 9. The essential dignities of the planets

We leap from page 275 to page 284 literally and metaphorically, for here Crowley includes the outer planets Uranus, Neptune, and Pluto with the Lunar Nodes in their Exaltation and Fall.

Tables of the Tarot

Aleister Crowley makes no comment about these tables, which is always suspicious. In one respect the information is simply a tabulation of what has already been established, but there are anomalies.

The major Arcana

Page 278. Important Kabbalistic and numerical attributions related to the Key Scale in *777*.

Apart from the mess that is the Key Scale column which begs to be put back in order, the eye is drawn to the final two rows, which have no attribution to the Major Arcana. Of course, we know The Aeon and the Universe perform double duty with Fire and Spirit, and Saturn and Earth, respectively, but 32 bis and 31 bis are treated differently. The clue to their true importance is seen in Table II of *777* where they are associated with the Princesses and the Aces. The sum of the letters YHShVH (Jesus) is 326, which Crowley directs us to 300, which is Aeon, Shin expanded is 360 which we have already discussed. Another circle.

The harmonic of 8 is 80, Peh, Atu XVI, or Mars. When Peh is placed at the end of a word, it is 800, but there appears to be a typo in this table: Pe 80,000—Crowley is not so careless with the other final letters. Triple zero is a Trinity, naturally, and refers to the Supernals.

Returning to 32 bis and 31 bis on separate lines, they are effectively separate cards, which added to 78 gives 80. It is worth noting that the tables of the Court Cards on page 28 omit the Key Scale. (I am not suggesting that there should be 80 cards in a tarot deck—quite the opposite.) One meaning of 326 is ChSRVN, defect or want.

While we leap about, the pentagrams on page 275 might be consulted, for 5 is the number of Mars.

The two values of Peh make 880, and with 8, the number of Cheth we get 888, Jesus in Greek. Aleph, which contains Peh is 111, multiplied by 8 is 888. 888/3 is 296, HARTz. 888 is Ta-Nich, which Crowley enumerates as 78. See *The Temple of Solomon* Part 6 which includes an Invocation of Horus as well as an account of how the Stele of Revealing was discovered.

The number 88 is ChNKY, initiation into the Mysteries, see *AL*, I. 46, and see the *Mysteries of the Qabalah*, Part 2 The Apocalypse, Chapter 88.

Ta-nich is 370, the Liber of which concerns sex magick.

Crowley gives a detailed breakdown of *Liber Israfel* in *Book IV*, Part 3

- *Liber 370* commentary: the phallus
- The Formulae of the Elemental Weapons analysis of Liber Israfel
- Moonchild
- *Liber 6* attributions and instructions
- *Liber 8* preparation of the temple
- *Liber 9* section on physical clairvoyance using tarot cards
- *Liber NU* more on ritual

The four scales of colour

Page 279 to 281. Crowley dithered on whether to use the Golden Dawn titles or his own. In the end he plumped for Knight, Queen, Prince, and Princess in Tetragrammaton order.

6. For Key Scale 11 to 31 bis
7. For Key Scale 1 to 10

The colour scales conceal powerful magical formulae.

Celestial dominion of the court cards

Page 282. See Table II of *777*. As the note to the Princess states, the corresponding Ace ruling a quadrant around the North Pole is included. Crowley's system is using the *Book T* system rather than the complicated version created by Mathers. See page 283.

Titles and attributions of the small cards

Page 283. See *Book T*. Crowley changed some of the titles found in *Book T*. The Aces have part of their title, 'The Root of the Power of ...', while in *Book T* the title format is 'The Root of the Powers of the ...' Clearly the Aces belong in the table on page 282. The Svastika, whose form is similar to Aleph, The Fool, and to Mars is here represented.

The table presents the small cards in the familiar format of the Sephiroth on the Tree of Life.

The Holy trinity

The sacredness of the Trinity expressed as God, the Father, and the Holy Spirit.

The essential dignities of the planets

Page 284. The Zodiac wheel at the top essentially presents the same information as the table below it.

The planets ruling the signs of the Zodiac are traditional, i.e. Mars rules Aries, Venus rules Taurus, etc. A planet in detriment is in the sign of opposite ruling, so Mars in Libra is detriment, Venus in Scorpio is detriment, and so on.

The final unnamed column is the Key Scale with Aries 28 transposed with Aquarius 15.

Exaltation is the strongest place for each planet; this is traditional. However Crowley includes the outer planets and the lunar nodes to fill the gaps (a planet can only be in exaltation in one sign). The same planet in the same degree of the opposing sign is in its Fall, and therefore at its weakest.

Crowley also gives rulership of the outer planets to the signs.

Herschel (Uranus) rules the 4 Kerubic Signs.

Neptune rules the 4 Fixed Signs and exalted in Aquarius. Aquarius is an air sign, but its name suggests water.

Therefore we would expect Pluto to rule the cardinal signs, but instead Crowley assigns the Primum Mobile, which is Kether. Kether is expressed as Chokmah, which is also associated with the whirling of the circle of the Zodiac. The secret attribution of Chokmah is Atu I; Mercury takes on the characteristics of the aspecting planets and Zodiac sign.

The triple trinity of the planets

Page 285. And see *Liber 777*, page 47. The Triple Trinity requires the outer planets Uranus and Neptune—Pluto is omitted. As Crowley suggests, 'intellectual' should be replaced with 'conscious'.
The horizontal components are:

- The Self—(Ego) is alchemical Mercury Will of the Self is alchemical Sulphur Relation with the non-ego is alchemical Earth.
- 'Non-Ego' is Jung's collective unconscious.
- The Middle Pillar is Consciousness, corresponding to the Self—(Ego). The Pillar of Mercy is the 'Mode of action on the non-ego', which is the unconscious. The Pillar of Severity is the 'Mode of Self-expression'.

The title of this page gives us another clue, for 3 × 3 = 9, which can be the Square of Saturn, or the AYQ BKR table. The Trinity of 000 is naturally omitted but see Peh on page 278.
The Self and the Middle Pillar have identical planetary rulers, but with Luna having different attributions ('The Sensory' and 'The Automatic').
Below are suggested meanings from Crowley's writings.

The spiritual

> The spiritual planes are of several types, but are all distinguished by a reality and intensity to be found nowhere else. Their inhabitants are formless, free of space and time, and distinguished by incomparable brilliance.
>
> (*Book IV*, Part 3)

Reaching the spiritual plane is dualistic, travelling through angels and demons alike.

The intellectual

The intellectual plane or world:

> The number Four, Chesed, is here manifested in the realm of the Intellect. Chesed refers to Jupiter who rules in Libra in this decanate. The sum of

these symbols is therefore without opposition; hence the card proclaims the idea of authority in the intellectual world. It is the establishment of dogma, and law concerning it. It represents a refuge from mental chaos, chosen in an arbitrary manner. It argues for convention.

(4 of Swords, *Book of Thoth*)

The sensory

The world we live in, embodiment, using our senses.

The automatic

See sensory.

The creative

Masculine, phallic, the Will. See 2 of Wands.

The paternal

The Father (Atu IV) and Atu IX. Chesed. AD is the paternal formula, Hadit.

The passionate

> May the **passionate** *'love under will' which she has stored in this Trea-sury of Truth and Beauty flow forth from the Splendour and Strength of her work to enlighten the world; may this Tarot serve as a chart for the bold seamen of the New Aeon, to guide them across the Great Sea of Under-standing to the City of the Pyramids!*

(*Book of Thoth*)

The intuitive

> *The RUACH is centred in the airy Sephira, Tiphareth, who is the Son, the first-born of the Father, and the Sun, the first emanation of the creative Phallus. He derives directly from his mother Binah through the Path of Zain, the sublime **intuitive** sense, so that he partakes absolutely of the nature of Neschamah. From his father, Chokmah, he is informed though*

the Path of Heh', the Great Mother, the Star, our Lady Nuit, so that the
creative impulse is communicated to him by all possibilities soever.

(Ace of Swords, *Book of Thoth*)

The volitional

Intentional action. However, these actions may not be under control, so
Crowley suggests using The Scourge, The Dagger, and the Chain; The
Wand; The Pantacle (*Book IV*, Part 2).

> *Instead of condemning the three qualities outright, we should consider*
> *them as parts of a sacrament. This particular aspect of the Scourge, the*
> *Dagger, and the Chain, suggests the sacrament of penance.*
>
> *The Scourge is Sulphur: its application excites our sluggish natures;*
> *and it may further be used as an instrument of correction, to castigate*
> *rebellious volitions. It is applied to the Nephesh, the Animal Soul, the*
> *natural desires.*
>
> *The Dagger is Mercury: it is used to calm too great heat, by the letting*
> *of blood; and it is this weapon which is plunged into the side or heart of*
> *the Magician to fill the Holy Cup. Those faculties which come between the*
> *appetites and the reason are thus dealt with.*
>
> *The Chain is Salt: it serves to bind the wandering thoughts; and for*
> *this reason is placed about the neck of the Magician, where Daath is*
> *situated.*
>
> *These instruments also remind us of pain, death, and bondage.*
> *Students of the gospel will recollect that in the martyrdom of Christ these*
> *three were used, the dagger being replaced by the nails.*

Note these alchemical qualities of Salt, Mercury, and Sulphur appear in
the upper section.

The triplicities of the Zodiac

Page 286. Expressed as signs of the Zodiac as they relate to the Court
Cards. The descriptions are alchemical and they derive from Masonic
sources.

Appended to the system as Malkuth are the Princesses as the Thrones
of Spirit who naturally leap up to Kether.

The vital Triads

Page 287 and *Liber 777*, page 41. Seven sets of Triads with the Universe appended. The Study of *Liber Trigrammaton* is recommended.

The Three Gods IAO

- The Fool
- The Magus
- The Hermit

Three Gods:

> *Intoxication, that is, ecstasy, is the Key to Reality. It is explained in Energized Enthusiasm The Equinox 9 that there are three Gods whose function is to bring the Soul to the Realization of its own glory: Dionysus, Aphrodite, Apollo; Wine, Woman, and Song.*
>
> (*AL*, I.63)

> *These three Gods are Dionysus, Apollo, Aphrodite. In English: wine, woman and song.*
>
> (*Liber 811*)

The Three Goddesses

- The High Priestess
- The Empress
- The Star

The Three Demiurges

- Fortune
- The Emperor
- The Hermit

> *The Demiurge is the divine Will, attributed to Chesed.*
> *Also the purity was divided by Strength, the force of the Demiurge.*
> (*Liber Trigrammaton*)

The Children Horus and Hoor-Pa-Kraat

- The Lovers
- The Sun
- The Tower

The Yoni Gaudens (The Woman Satisfied)

- The Chariot
- Art
- Adjustment

See Crowley's commentary on Atu VIII.

The Slain Gods

- Lust
- The Hanged Man
- Death

The Mass of the Holy Ghost

The Lingam, The Yoni, The Stele (Priest, Priestess, Ceremony)

- The Devil
- The Moon
- Aeon

The Gnostic Mass.

The Pantacle of the Whole

- The Universe

The final Heh of the Formula of Tetragrammaton.

PART THREE

THE *BOOK OF THOTH* AND
THE *BOOK OF THE LAW*

CHAPTER TWELVE

Liber AL vel Legis

For Thelemites, *Liber AL* 'solves' a problem that does not exist, namely *AL*, I.57, while Crowley liberally sprinkles verses throughout the *Book of Thoth*, particularly in the Atu. The problem is that if *Liber AL* is so important, then Crowley would have anchored this book with the Tarot. Crowley does exactly that in an interesting way.

The clue is found in the 'Bibliographical Note' where he claims the 'Naples Arrangement' is one of his greatest achievements. For the most part of the 'Naples Arrangement' he is expanding on the geometry and numbers that are part of the Masonic system, but primarily inspired by Kant.

Where he deviates is in assigning Netzach, Hod, and Yesod to Bliss, Thought, and Being, in the normal Sanskrit order, Sat, Chit, Ananda, fulfilled in Malkuth. This is another example of the Daughter coming from another source.

The key to understanding why Crowley identifies these sephiroth to Sat, Chit, Ananda is found in his Old and New Comment on the first verse in *Liber AL*.

Nu is 56, precursor to 7, 8, and 9, and it is the number of the Minor Arcana and Court Cards. 56 + 9 = 65, Adonai, the Lord, whose is expansion is 671, TARO. Adonai is Solar but 65 is a number sacred to Mars.

Nu is related to On, Noah, Oannes, Jonah, John, Dianus, and Diana (see Atu XIII); Mars rules Scorpio.

Had is 10, added to Nu is 66, the sum of 1 to 11 and the centre of ABRAHADABRA. Abrahadabra is intimately related to Cheth (chit), Atu VII and *Liber 418*. Crowley says Had is Set (Sat).

Ananda is missing from Crowley's analysis. Furthermore, his ordering of Sat, Chit, Ananda is reversed in The 'Naples Arrangement'.

Contemplation of 7, 8, and 9, reveals connections to *Liber 231* and the *Book of Lies* that otherwise remain mysterious.

The numbers 7 and 8 represent the base of the Pillars of Yachin and Boaz in the Temple of Solomon, and, of course, sum of the Tarot. The sum of 7, 8, and 9 is 24, an important number of the Apocalypse.

Crowley defines 9 as 'itself fulfilled in its complement'. The sum of any number multiplied by 9 is always 9, another example of the circle, which is good when considered as 3 × 3 which takes us to Binah. However, this too can be a trap.

9 × 9 is 81, the number of IAO, important in higher Masonic levels. The sum of 81 takes us back to 9. The solution is with appending 1 to the 9 in Malkuth, or the Daughter, otherwise known as 10. The mystery of *Liber 231* can now be solved. The sigils for Tau appended at the base of the column (Malkuth) in both cases are IAO and ADNY, respectively. Adonai is the Redeemer, while IAO is circular – it needs an extra letter.

In this format IAO represents an association with Black Brothers, Crowley's codeword for Mathers' Golden Dawn. The problem with Mathers' system is that it goes nowhere for the students – the idea being, of course, that the solution is to fill Mathers pockets. The two columns of 22 letter-sigils juxtapose IAO with ADNY.

The *Book of Lies* is such a Mercurial name, and its number is 333 which sum to 9: three sets of triads. The number of chapters is 91, ten more than IAO. 91 is Amen, which completes a prayer.

Summary

Analysis of the first verse of *Liber AL* gives the complete system that unites the TARO with The 'Naples Arrangement' using Sat, Chit, Ananda – this is his 'greatest achievement'.

Furthermore, he compares and contrasts the 'old' system of Mathers with his 'new' system presented in *Liber 231* and the solution using the Formula of the Tetragrammaton and the *Book of Lies*.

Uniting Liber 220 with The Book of Thoth

220 suggests a simple matrix of 22 Atu × 10 sephiroth using the order of the Atu from the *Book of Thoth*. The ordinal number of the verses from 1 to 220 has kabbalistic and gematria attributions to be explored.

Liber 220, Chapter 1

Verse XI on page 257 is a paraphrase of verses from the *Book of the Law* complete with a reference to *Liber 418* which requires further investigation. The omission of the *Book of the Law* from the *Book of Thoth* is curious, and therefore it necessary to redress the balance.

Significance is indicated by repetition, in an efficient manner. For example, Thelema appears only once as does 418, but 418 is repeated in the title. Abrahadabra appears several times. However, in the various commentaries written by Crowley, 418 and Abrahadabra are common themes.

0 The Fool

1 Kether – Had! The manifestation of Nuit.

See ARN, *Liber 418*.

THE CRY OF THE HAWK
Hoor hath a secret fourfold name: it is Do What Thou Wilt. Four Words: Naught – One – Many – All. Thou – Child! Thy Name is holy. Thy Kingdom is come. Thy Will is done. Here is the Bread. Here is the Blood. Bring us through Temptation! Deliver us from Good and Evil! That Mine as Thine be the Crown of the Kingdom, even now. ABRAHADABRA. These ten words are four, the Name of the One.

COMMENTARY
The 'Hawk' referred to is Horus.
The chapter begins with a comment on Liber Legis III, 49.
Those four words, 'Do What Thou Wilt', are also identified with the four possible modes of conceiving the Universe; Horus unites these.
Follows a version of the 'Lord's Prayer', suitable to Horus. Compare this with the version in Chapter 44. There are ten sections in this prayer, and, as the prayer is attributed to Horus, they are called four, as above

explained; but it is only the name of Horus which is fourfold; He himself is One.

This may be compared with the Qabalistic doctrine of the Ten Sephiroth as an expression of Tetragrammaton (1 + 2 + 3 + 4 = 10).

It is now seen that this Hawk is not Solar, but Mercurial; hence the words, the Cry of the Hawk, the essential part of Mercury being his Voice; and the number of the Chapter, B, which is Beth the letter of Mercury, the Magus of the Tarot, who has four weapons, and it must be remembered that this card is numbered 1, again connecting all these symbols with the Phallus. The essential weapon of Mercury is the Caduceus.

(Book of Lies)

Clearly this chapter of the *Book of Lies* is a commentary on the first verse which links it to Atu I and Mercury.

Had as the point is a Kantian thing-in-itself. Nuit is space.

2 Chokmah – The unveiling of the company of heaven.

Traditionally Chokmah is the zodiac or heavens revealed from Kether.

3 Binah – Every man and every woman is a star.

Stars are things-in-themselves.

4 Chesed – Every number is infinite; there is no difference.

Numbers are things-in-themselves, points of light.

5 Geburah – Help me, o warrior lord of Thebes, in my unveiling before the Children of men!

Things-in-themselves in space. Warrior – Geburah.

6 Tipareth – Be thou Hadit, my secret centre, my heart & my tongue!

Union with the thing-in-itself who is one's Holy Guardian Angel.

7 Netzach – Behold! it is revealed by Aiwass the minister of Hoor-paar-kraat.

8 Hod – The Khabs is in the Khu, not the Khu in the Khabs.

9 Yesod – Worship then the Khabs, and behold my light shed over you!

Lunar Light and Darkness, duality. See 2 of Disks which cites the lineages of TARO Masters. A further development of the technique in verse 6.

10 Malkuth – Let my servants be few & secret: they shall rule the many & the known.
Malkuth is the influence from a strange quarter which rules.

I The Magus

11 Kether – These are fools that men adore; both their Gods & their men are fools.
Two Fools, but this verse is ruled by Atu I in Kether, therefore 0 = 2.

12 Chokmah – Come forth, o children, under the stars, & take your fill of love!
Union of Duality. See *Liber Aleph*. Chokmah represents the zodiac.

13 Binah – I am above you and in you. My ecstasy is in yours. My joy is to see your joy.
Mystical Union.

14 Chesed – Above, the gemmèd azure is The naked splendour of Nuit; She bends in ecstasy to kiss The secret ardours of Hadit. The winged globe, the starry blue, Are mine, O Ankh-af-na-khonsu!
'Winged Globe' cited extensively throughout Crowley's writings as an object of meditation.

15 Geburah – Now ye shall know that the chosen priest & apostle of infinite space is the prince-priest the Beast; and in his woman called the Scarlet Woman is all power given. They shall gather my children into their fold: they shall bring the glory of the stars into the hearts of men.
The union of Tipareth and Geburah. Beast and Scarlet Woman often refer to individuals, but Crowley says they can also be titles. The Secret Key to this verse is Abrahadabra. The sum of the verse 6 – 5 is Adeptus Minor and Adeptus Major. See also 2 of Disks.

16 Tipareth – For he is ever a sun, and she a moon. But to him is the winged secret flame, and to her the stooping starlight.
Expression of duality experienced differently by male and female.

17 Netzach – But ye are not so chosen.

18 Hod – Burn upon their brows, o splendrous serpent!
The serpent is a symbol of Mercury as the Caduceus.

19 Yesod – O azure-lidded woman, bend upon them!

20 Malkuth – The key of the rituals is in the secret word which I have given unto him.
The secret word is Abrahadabra.

II The High Priestess

21 Kether – With the God & the Adorer I am nothing: they do not see me. They are as upon the earth; I am Heaven, and there is no other God than me, and my lord Hadit.
The High Priestess traverses the path from Tipareth to Kether, the point (Hadit).

22 Chokmah – Now, therefore, I am known to ye by my name Nuit, and to him by a secret name which I will give him when at last he knoweth me. Since I am Infinite Space, and the Infinite Stars thereof, do ye also thus. Bind nothing! Let there be no difference made among you between any one thing & any other thing; for thereby there cometh hurt.
Chokmah as the stars and space known by Nuit and Isis. Space is 'no difference' between the points.

23 Binah – But whoso availeth in this, let him be the chief of all!
'All' is 61 AYN or nothing. The key to rulership.

24 Chesed – I am Nuit, and my word is six and fifty.
65, Adonai expanded is 671 the number of TARO.

25 Geburah – Divide, add, multiply, and understand.
This exercise is achieved in the previous verse.

26 Tipareth – Then saith the prophet and slave of the beauteous one: Who am I, and what shall be the sign? So she answered him, bending down, a lambent flame of blue, all-touching, all penetrant, her lovely hands upon the black earth, & her lithe body arched for love, and her soft feet not hurting the little flowers: Thou knowest! And the sign

shall be my ecstasy, the consciousness of the continuity of existence, the omnipresence of my body.

6 of Cups, Beauty.

27 Netzach – Then the priest answered & said unto the Queen of Space, kissing her lovely brows, and the dew of her light bathing his whole body in a sweet-smelling perfume of sweat: O Nuit, continuous one of Heaven, let it be ever thus; that men speak not of Thee as One but as None; and let them speak not of thee at all, since thou art continuous!

28 Hod – None, breathed the light, faint & faery, of the stars, and two.

Analysis of 0 = 2. Later, Crowley realised the stars, Chokmah is ruled by Mercury.

29 Yesod – For I am divided for love's sake, for the chance of union.

Further analysis of *solve et coagula*.

30 Malkuth – This is the creation of the world, that the pain of division is as nothing, and the joy of dissolution all.

Malkuth – the world, which is separate from the other sephiroth.

III The Empress

31 Kether – For these fools of men and their woes care not thou at all! They feel little; what is, is balanced by weak joys; but ye are my chosen ones.

The sense of feeling is feminine.

32 Chokmah – Obey my prophet! follow out the ordeals of my knowledge! seek me only! Then the joys of my love will redeem ye from all pain. This is so: I swear it by the vault of my body; by my sacred heart and tongue; by all I can give, by all I desire of ye all.

Chokmah is an aspect of knowledge and wisdom. Note the three zeros in the final sentence.

33 Binah – Then the priest fell into a deep trance or swoon, & said unto the Queen of Heaven; Write unto us the ordeals; write unto us the rituals; write unto us the law!

Binah is the natural home of the Queen. Ordeals, Rituals, Law.

34 Chesed – But she said: the ordeals I write not: the rituals shall be half known and half concealed: the Law is for all.

Chesed, the natural home of law and order. Ordeals, Rituals, Law in terms of duality to be united – *solve et coagula*.

35 Geburah – This that thou writest is the threefold book of Law.

The vital triad of the *Book of the Law* expressed as force.

36 Tipareth – My scribe Ankh-af-na-khonsu, the priest of the princes, shall not in one letter change this book; but lest there be folly, he shall comment thereupon by the wisdom of Ra-Hoor-Khuit.

Tipareth, the natural place of the Princes.

37 Netzach – Also the mantras and spells; the obeah and the wanga; the work of the wand and the work of the sword; these he shall learn and teach.

Netzach, the Shakti gives power to the mantras and spells.

38 Hod – He must teach; but he may make severe the ordeals.

Hod is on the Pillar of Severity.

39 Yesod – The word of the Law is Θελημα.

Thelema.

40 Malkuth – Who calls us Thelemites will do no wrong, if he look but close into the word. For there are therein Three Grades, the Hermit, and the Lover, and the man of Earth. Do what thou wilt shall be the whole of the Law.

Malkuth – 'the man of Earth'. The Hermit and Lover, Virgo and Gemini, respectively, are ruled by Mercury. Man is 91, Amen, and the number of chapters in the *Book of Lies*.

IV The *Emperor*

41 Kether – The word of Sin is Restriction. O man! refuse not thy wife, if she will! O lover, if thou wilt, depart! There is no bond that can unite the divided but love: all else is a curse. Accursed! Accursed be it to the aeons! Hell.

41 is 'AM, the Mother, unfertilised and unenlightened,' and 'The yoni as a vampire force, sterile.'

42 Chokmah – Let it be that state of manyhood bound and loathing. So with thy all; thou hast no right but to do thy will.

42 AMA, the Mother, still dark. Here are the 42 judges of the dead in Amennti, and here is the 42-fold name of the Creative God. See Liber 418.

(Liber 58)

43 Binah – Do that, and no other shall say nay.

43 A number of orgasm – especially the male.

(Liber 58)

'Nay' is 61, an aspect of Nothing.

44 Chesed – For pure will, unassuaged of purpose, delivered from the lust of result, is every way perfect.
See 'the Mass of the Phoenix'.

45 Geburah – The Perfect and the Perfect are one Perfect and not two; nay, are none!
'Nay' see verse 43 above. Peh, The Tower is 80, ruled by Mars.

46 Tipareth – Nothing is a secret key of this law. Sixty-one the Jews call it; I call it eight, eighty, four hundred & eighteen.
Note the predominance of 8. 418 see *The Vision and the Voice*.

47 Netzach – But they have the half: unite by thine art so that all disappear.
See Art Atu XIV.

48 Hod – My prophet is a fool with his one, one, one; are not they the Ox, and none by the Book?
Atu 0. Aleph is ALP, 111. The *Book of TARO*.

49 Yesod – Abrogate are all rituals, all ordeals, all words and signs. Ra-Hoor-Khuit hath taken his seat in the East at the Equinox of the Gods; and let Asar be with Isa, who also are one. But they are not of me. Let Asar be the adorant, Isa the sufferer; Hoor in his secret name and splendour is the Lord initiating.
This verse refers to the dissolution of the old system (Mathers) based upon degree-mongering with Crowley's system based upon initiation. Isa is Jesus, while the verse number refers to Venus and the Sigil of the A∴A∴ Verse 48 is Atu 0, therefore this verse is Atu I, The Magus.

50 Kether – There is a word to say about the Hierophantic task. Behold! there are three ordeals in one, and it may be given in three ways. The gross must pass through fire; let the fine be tried in intellect, and the lofty chosen ones in the highest. Thus ye have star & star, system & system; let not one know well the other!

The verse number refers to Atu XIII Death, the word of Initiation.

The Hierophant

The Hierophant appears in the previous verse as an Initiate

51 Kether – There are four gates to one palace; the floor of that palace is of silver and gold; lapis lazuli & jasper are there; and all rare scents; jasmine & rose, and the emblems of death. Let him enter in turn or at once the four gates; let him stand on the floor of the palace. Will he not sink? Amn. Ho! warrior, if thy servant sink? But there are means and means. Be goodly therefore: dress ye all in fine apparel; eat rich foods and drink sweet wines and wines that foam! Also, take your fill and will of love as ye will, when, where and with whom ye will! But always unto me.

Malkuth is in Kether after another way.

52 Chokmah – If this be not aright; if ye confound the space-marks, saying: They are one; or saying, They are many; if the ritual be not ever unto me: then expect the direful judgments of Ra-Hoor-Khuit!

Chokmah as space: 'space-marks'.

Ra-Hoor-Khuit: Atu XVI.

53 Binah – This shall regenerate the world, the little world my sister, my heart & my tongue, unto whom I send this kiss. Also, o scribe and prophet, though thou be of the princes, it shall not assuage thee nor absolve thee. But ecstasy be thine and joy of earth: ever To me! To me!

'This shall regenerate the world', the A∴A∴

54 Chesed – Change not as much as the style of a letter; for behold! thou, o prophet, shalt not behold all these mysteries hidden therein.

Chesed is the perfect expression of stability.

55 Geburah – The child of thy bowels, he shall behold them.

The verse number is that of Malkuth and the Princess who arrives from another place of manifestation.

56 Tipareth – Expect him not from the East, nor from the West; for from no expected house cometh that child. Aum! All words are sacred and all prophets true; save only that they understand a little; solve the first half of the equation, leave the second unattacked. But thou hast all in the clear light, and some, though not all, in the dark.

The Grade of Magus. Nu is 56, while Tipareth is the place of the child. 'Clear light', the Sun.

57 Netzach – Invoke me under my stars! Love is the law, love under will. Nor let the fools mistake love; for there are love and love. There is the dove, and there is the serpent. Choose ye well! He, my prophet, hath chosen, knowing the law of the fortress, and the great mystery of the House of God. All these old letters of my Book are aright; but Tzaddi is not the Star. This also is secret: my prophet shall reveal it to the wise.

See *Liber Nu.*

58 Hod – I give unimaginable joys on earth: certainty, not faith, while in life, upon death; peace unutterable, rest, ecstasy; nor do I demand aught in sacrifice.

Master of the Temple.

59 Yesod – My incense is of resinous woods & gums; and there is no blood therein: because of my hair the trees of Eternity.

Knowledge of Nuit and *The Star Sponge Vision.*

60 Malkuth – My number is 11, as all their numbers who are of us. The Five Pointed Star, with a Circle in the Middle, & the circle is Red. My colour is black to the blind, but the blue & gold are seen of the seeing. Also I have a secret glory for them that love me.

Liber Nu.

VI The Lovers

61 Kether – But to love me is better than all things: if under the night stars in the desert thou presently burnest mine incense before me, invoking me with a pure heart, and the Serpent flame therein, thou shalt come a little to lie in my bosom. For one kiss wilt thou then be willing to give all; but whoso gives one particle of dust shall lose all in that hour. Ye shall gather goods and store of women and spices; ye shall wear rich jewels; ye shall exceed the nations of the earth in

splendour & pride; but always in the love of me, and so shall ye come to my joy. I charge you earnestly to come before me in a single robe, and covered with a rich headdress. I love you! I yearn to you! Pale or purple, veiled or voluptuous, I who am all pleasure and purple, and drunkenness of the innermost sense, desire you. Put on the wings, and arouse the coiled splendour within you: come unto me!

A Ritual of *Liber NV.*

62 Chokmah – At all my meetings with you shall the priestess say – and her eyes shall burn with desire as she stands bare and rejoicing in my secret temple – To me! To me! calling forth the flame of the hearts of all in her love-chant.

The Secret Temple, possibly the 'living Temple', page 48.

63 Binah – Sing the rapturous love-song unto me! Burn to me perfumes! Wear to me jewels! Drink to me, for I love you! I love you!

64 Chesed – I am the blue-lidded daughter of Sunset; I am the naked brilliance of the voluptuous night-sky.

64, a number of Mercury.

65 Geburah – To me! To me!

Adonai, the Lord.

66 Tipareth – The Manifestation of Nuit is at an end.

Liber 220 Chapter 2

Chapter 2 starts half way through Atu VI.

67 Netzach – 1 Nu! the hiding of Hadit.

67 BINH the Great Mother. Note 6 + 7 = 13, uniting the ideas of Binah and Kether. A number of the aspiration.

67 The womb of the mother containing the twins.

67 is Zain, a Sword, the letter of The Lovers.

68 Hod – 2 Come! all ye, and learn the secret that hath not yet been revealed. I, Hadit, am the complement of Nu, my bride. I am not extended, and Khabs is the name of my House.

69 Yesod – 3 In the sphere I am everywhere the centre, as she, the circumference, is nowhere found.

3, 6, and 9

70 Malkuth – 4 Yet she shall be known & I never.
70 is Ayin, nothing, while Malkuth is the full manifestation. 70 is also The Devil, another expression of the full manifestation.

VII The Chariot

71 Kether – 5 Behold! the rituals of the old time are black. Let the evil ones be cast away; let the good ones be purged by the prophet! Then shall this Knowledge go aright.
A reference to Mathers system of the Golden Dawn. The Chariot is Cheth, 418; see *The Vision and the Voice*.

72 Chokmah – 6 I am the flame that burns in every heart of man, and in the core of every star. I am Life, and the giver of Life, yet therefore is the knowledge of me the knowledge of death.
Death – Initiation.

73 Binah – 7 I am the Magician and the Exorcist. I am the axle of the wheel, and the cube in the circle. 'Come unto me' is a foolish word: for it is I that go.
Atus II, X, XXI, 0.
'To go', the power of the Sphinx.

74 Chesed – 8 Who worshipped Heru-pa-kraath have worshipped me; ill, for I am the worshipper.

75 Geburah – 9 Remember all ye that existence is pure joy; that all the sorrows are but as shadows; they pass & are done; but there is that which remains.
Sat, Chit, Ananda; see the 'Naples Arrangement'.

76 Tipareth – 10 O prophet! thou hast ill will to learn this writing.
Sorrow (3 of Swords) is a complex thread in the *Book of Thoth*.

77 Netzach – 11 I see thee hate the hand & the pen; but I am stronger.
77 is OZ The Goat.

78 Hod – 12 Because of me in Thee which thou knewest not.
The TARO.

79 Yesod – 13 for why? Because thou wast the knower, and me.
79 is the number of the Pillars of Yachin and Boaz.

80 Malkuth – 14 Now let there be a veiling of this shrine: now let the light devour men and eat them up with blindness!
Malkuth and Peh sum to 90 The Star.

VIII Adjustment

81 Kether – 15 For I am perfect, being Not; and my number is nine by the fools; but with the just I am eight, and one in eight: Which is vital, for I am none indeed. The Empress and the King are not of me; for there is a further secret.

With the just I am eight, and one in eight.

(Society of Eight)

81 is the square of 9.

82 Chokmah – 16 I am The Empress & the Hierophant. Thus eleven, as my bride is eleven.

83 Binah – 17 Hear me, ye people of sighing! The sorrows of pain and regret Are left to the dead and the dying, The folk that not know me as yet.

83 Consecration: love in its highest form: energy, freedom, amrita, aspiration. The root of the idea of romance plus religion.

(Liber 777)

84 Chesed – 18 These are dead, these fellows; they feel not. We are not for the poor and sad: the lords of the earth are our kinsfolk.

84 A number chiefly important in Buddhism. $84 = 7 \times 12$.

(Liber 777)

85 Geburah – 19 Is a God to live in a dog? No! but the highest are of us. They shall rejoice, our chosen: who sorroweth is not of us.
85 is the number of Peh, the mouth.

86 Tipareth – 20 Beauty and strength, leaping laughter and delicious languor, force and fire, are of us.
Tipareth – Beauty
Force and Fire. 86 is the number of the Pentagram.

87 Netzach – 21 We have nothing with the outcast and the unfit: let them die in their misery. For they feel not. Compassion is the vice of kings: stamp down the wretched & the weak: this is the law of the strong: this is our law and the joy of the world. Think not, o king, upon that lie: That Thou Must Die: verily thou shalt not die, but live. Now let it be understood: If the body of the King dissolve, he shall remain in pure ecstasy for ever. Nuit! Hadit! Ra-Hoor-Khuit! The Sun, Strength & Sight, Light; these are for the servants of the Star & the Snake.

88 Hod – 22 I am the Snake that giveth Knowledge & Delight and bright glory, and stir the hearts of men with drunkenness. To worship me take wine and strange drugs whereof I will tell my prophet, & be drunk thereof! They shall not harm ye at all. It is a lie, this folly against self. The exposure of innocence is a lie. Be strong, o man! lust, enjoy all things of sense and rapture: fear not that any God shall deny thee for this.

Netzach and Hod unified.

89 Yesod – 23 I am alone: there is no God where I am.

The Hanged Man.

90 Malkuth – 24 Behold! these be grave mysteries; for there are also of my friends who be hermits. Now think not to find them in the forest or on the mountain; but in beds of purple, caressed by magnificent beasts of women with large limbs, and fire and light in their eyes, and masses of flaming hair about them; there shall ye find them. Ye shall see them at rule, at victorious armies, at all the joy; and there shall be in them a joy a million times greater than this. Beware lest any force another, King against King! Love one another with burning hearts; on the low men trample in the fierce lust of your pride, in the day of your wrath.

Hermits – The Hermit.

IX The Hermit

91 Kether – 25 Ye are against the people, O my chosen!

91 is AMN. 25 is the number of Mars.

92 Chokmah – 26 I am the secret Serpent coiled about to spring: in my coiling there is joy. If I lift up my head, I and my Nuit are one.

If I droop down mine head, and shoot forth venom, then is rapture of the earth, and I and the earth are one.

93 Binah – 27 There is great danger in me; for who doth not understand these runes shall make a great miss. He shall fall down into the pit called Because, and there he shall perish with the dogs of Reason.

94 Chesed – 28 Now a curse upon Because and his kin!

95 Geburah – 29 May Because be accursed for ever!
Accursed, a function of Geburah.

96 Tipareth – 30 If Will stops and cries Why, invoking Because, then Will stops & does nought.
We are back on the central pillar.

97 Netzach – 31 If Power asks why, then is Power weakness.
Netzach – Power.

98 Hod – 32 Also reason is a lie; for there is a factor infinite & unknown; & all their words are skew-wise.
Reason – a function of Mercury.

99 Yesod – 33 Enough of Because! Be he damned for a dog!

100 Malkuth – 34 But ye, o my people, rise up & awake!

X Fortune

Fortune is the Atu of ritual.

101 Kether – 35 Let the rituals be rightly performed with joy & beauty!
101 is Joy. See the *Book of Lies*.

102 Chokmah – 36 There are rituals of the elements and feasts of the times.

103 Binah – 37 A feast for the first night of the Prophet and his Bride!
Binah is Saturn and the night.

104 Chesed – 38 A feast for the three days of the writing of the Book of the Law.

105 Geburah – 39 A feast for Tahuti and the child of the Prophet–secret, O Prophet!
Revealed in the *Book of Thoth*.

106 Tipareth – 40 A feast for the Supreme Ritual, and a feast for the Equinox of the Gods.

107 Netzach – 41 A feast for fire and a feast for water; a feast for life and a greater feast for death!

108 Hod – 42 A feast every day in your hearts in the joy of my rapture!
Daily invocation of Tahuti is an example.

109 Yesod – 43 A feast every night unto Nu, and the pleasure of uttermost delight!
See verse 42.

110 Malkuth – 44 'Aye! feast! rejoice! there is no dread hereafter. There is the dissolution, and eternal ecstasy in the kisses of Nu'.
Eight Feasts.

XI Lust

111 Kether – 45 There is death for the dogs.
111 – Liber Aleph.

112 Chokmah – 46 Dost thou fail? Art thou sorry? Is fear in thine heart?
46 is HBDLH, a dividing, sundering.

113 Binah – 47 Where I am these are not.
Above the Abyss.

114 Chesed – 48 Pity not the fallen! I never knew them. I am not for them. I console not: I hate the consoled & the consoler.
114 is DMO, a tear, the age of Christian Rozencreutz.

115 Geburah – 49 I am unique & conqueror. I am not of the slaves that perish. Be they damned & dead! Amen. (This is of the 4: there is a fifth who is invisible, & therein am I as a babe in an egg.)
Conqueror is an aspect of Mars.

116 Tipareth – 50 Blue am I and gold in the light of my bride: but the red gleam is in my eyes; & my spangles are purple & green.

117 Netzach – 51 Purple beyond purple: it is the light higher than eyesight.
Purple beyond purple is ultra-violet.

118 Hod – 52 There is a veil: that veil is black. It is the veil of the modest woman; it is the veil of sorrow, & the pall of death: this is none of me. Tear down that lying spectre of the centuries: veil not your vices in virtuous words: these vices are my service; ye do well, & I will reward you here and hereafter.

Hod – words. See *Liber Aleph*, 'On the Need for Declaring the Word'.

119 Yesod – 53 Fear not, o prophet, when these words are said, thou shalt not be sorry. Thou art emphatically my chosen; and blessed are the eyes that thou shalt look upon with gladness. But I will hide thee in a mask of sorrow: they that see thee shall fear thou art fallen: but I lift thee up.

119 DMOH, weeping.

120 Malkuth – 54 Nor shall they who cry aloud their folly that thou meanest nought avail; thou shall reveal it: thou availest: they are the slaves of because: They are not of me. The stops as thou wilt; the letters? change them not in style or value!

Atu 0.

Atu XII The Hanged Man

121 Kether – 55 Thou shalt obtain the order & value of the English Alphabet; thou shalt find new symbols to attribute them unto.

121 HGLGLYM, of swirling motions.

122 Chokmah – 56 Begone! ye mockers; even though ye laugh in my honour ye shall laugh not long: then when ye are sad know that I have forsaken you.

123 Binah – 57 He that is righteous shall be righteous still; he that is filthy shall be filthy still.

123 NGO plague; OGN to delay, hinder, or retard.

124 Chesed – 58 Yea! deem not of change: ye shall be as ye are, & not other. Therefore the kings of the earth shall be Kings for ever: the slaves shall serve. There is none that shall be cast down or lifted up: all is ever as it was. Yet there are masked ones my servants: it may be that yonder beggar is a King. A King may choose his garment as he will: there is no certain test: but a beggar cannot hide his poverty.

125 Geburah – 59 Beware therefore! Love all, lest perchance is a King concealed! Say you so? Fool! If he be a King, thou canst not hurt him.

Atu 0. 59 The yoni calling for the lingam as ovum, menstruum, or alkali.

126 Tipareth – 60 Therefore strike hard & low, and to hell with them, master!

127 Netzach – 61 There is a light before thine eyes, o prophet, a light undesired, most desirable.

128 Hod – 62 I am uplifted in thine heart; and the kisses of the stars rain hard upon thy body.

128 BVMP, lips.

129 Yesod – 63 Thou art exhaust in the voluptuous fullness of the inspiration; the expiration is sweeter than death, more rapid and laughterful than a caress of Hell's own worm.

Netzach – voluptuous.

130 Malkuth – 64 Oh! thou art overcome: we are upon thee; our delight is all over thee: hail! hail: prophet of Nu! prophet of Had! prophet of Ra-Hoor-Khu! Now rejoice! now come in our splendour & rapture! Come in our passionate peace, & write sweet words for the Kings.

64, the number of prophecy in the place of Malkuth.

XIII Death

The next ten verses pertain to trance.

131 Kether – 65 I am the Master: thou art the Holy Chosen One.

65 ADNY, Master.

131 is Pan.

132 Chokmah – 66 Write, & find ecstasy in writing! Work, & be our bed in working! Thrill with the joy of life & death! Ah! thy death shall be lovely: whoso seeth it shall be glad. Thy death shall be the seal of the promise of our age long love. Come! lift up thine heart & rejoice! We are one; we are none.

133 Binah – 67 Hold! Hold! Bear up in thy rapture; fall not in swoon of the excellent kisses!

Swoon – a trance, the basis of initiation = Death.

134 Chesed – 68 Harder! Hold up thyself! Lift thine head! breathe not so deep – die!
Die!

135 Geburah – 69 Ah! Ah! What do I feel? Is the word exhausted?

136 Tipareth – 70 There is help & hope in other spells. Wisdom says: be strong! Then canst thou bear more joy. Be not animal; refine thy rapture! If thou drink, drink by the eight and ninety rules of art: if thou love, exceed by delicacy; and if thou do aught joyous, let there be subtlety therein!
136, a Mystic Number of Jupiter, Taurus, and Vau.

137 Netzach – 71 But exceed! Exceed!
Netzach applying force.

138 Hod – 72 Strive ever to more! and if thou art truly mine – and doubt it not, an if thou art ever joyous! – death is the crown of all.
The Number of the 72 Names.

139 Yesod – 73 Ah! Ah! Death! Death! thou shalt long for death. Death is forbidden, o man, unto thee.
Three Deaths. 73 is the number of Gimel, The Priestess of the Silver Star, the female initiator and Chokmah, the Logos or male initiator.
'73 The feminine aspect of Chokmah in his phallic function' *Liber 777.*

140 Malkuth – 74 The length of thy longing shall be the strength of its glory. He that lives long & desires death much is ever the King among the Kings.

> *Blessed be She, ay, blessed unto the Ages be Our Lady Babalon, that plieth her scourge upon me, TO MEΓA θHPION, to compel me to creation and to destruction, which are one, in birth and in death, being Love!*
>
> *(Liber Aleph)*

XIV Art

141 Kether – 75 Aye! listen to the numbers & the words:
Applying the Atu and sephiroth to the verses.

142 Chokmah – 76. 4 6 3 8 A B K 2 4 A L G M O R 3 Y X 24 89 R P S T O V A L. What meaneth this, o prophet? Thou knowest not; nor shalt thou know ever. There cometh one to follow thee: he shall expound it.

But remember, o chose none, to be me; to follow the love of Nu in the star-lit heaven; to look forth upon men, to tell them this glad word. See 'The Cry of the Hawk', the *Book of Lies*.

143 Binah – 77 O be thou proud and mighty among men!
OZ – Strength.

144 Chesed – 78 Lift up thyself! for there is none like unto thee among men or among Gods! Lift up thyself, o my prophet, thy stature shall surpass the stars. They shall worship thy name, foursquare, mystic, wonderful, the number of the man; and the name of thy house 418. Compare with XI, page 257.

> 144. A square and therefore a materialisation of the number 12. Hence the numbers in the Apocalypse. 144,000 only means 12 (the perfect number in the Zodiac or houses of heaven and tribes of Israel) × 12, i.e. settled × 1000, i.e. on the grand scale.
>
> *(Liber 777)*

'Foursquare', a 4 × 4 square comprising the letters TARO.
418 see 'The Vision and the Voice'.

145 Geburah – 79 The end of the hiding of Hadit; and blessing & worship to the prophet of the lovely Star!

Liber 220, Chapter 3

146 Tipareth – 1 Abrahadabra; the reward of Ra-Hoor-Khuit.
Note that Chapter 2 commences half way through The Lovers, while Chapter 3 starts half way through Art. Both Atu are linked primarily through their alchemical attributions. This is not coincidence.
SVP, 146, limit, end, boundless. See the Naples Arrangement.
The union of IAO and Adonai.

147 Netzach – 2 There is division hither homeward; there is a word not known. Spelling is defunct; all is not aught. Beware! Hold! Raise the spell of Ra-Hoor-Khuit!
Geburah is the sephirah of division.

> *The Four Names in the Lesser Ritual of the Pentagram YHVH ADNY AHYH AGLA.*
>
> *(Liber 777)*

148 Hod – 3 Now let it be first understood that I am a god of War and of Vengeance. I shall deal hardly with them.

148 primarily deals with MAZNYM, Libra, which creates balance, particularly in the chakras which follow. Netzach Venus rules Libra.

149 Yesod – 4 Choose ye an island!

Presumably start with the base chakra and work upwards to the crown chakra.

150 Malkuth – 5 Fortify it!

150, *A Sandal*, NQ, innocent, purified.

XV The Devil

The Atu number reflects the previous verse.

151 Kether – 6 Dung it about with enginery of war!

151 is AHYH spelt in full. The 5 at the centre is Mars. The base chakra with the organs of elimination.

152 Chokmah – 7 I will give you a war-engine.

See *Liber Aleph*, 'The Nature of the Sphinx'. The following verses of Atu XV refer to the balancing of the four elements in Spirit, i.e. The Pentagram.

153 Binah – 8 With it ye shall smite the peoples; and none shall stand before you.

Verses 4–8 describe focusing on one of chakras, excluding all extraneous thoughts as a method of defence and strength.

'Smite' 153 is the number of Zain, a sword.

154 Chesed – 9 Lurk! Withdraw! Upon them! this is the Law of the Battle of Conquest: thus shall my worship be about my secret house.

Study *Liber HHH*.

SVD, secret is 70 Ayin, the letter of Atu XV. House is BYTh, Mercury. Combined we have 72 the number of The NAME.

155 Geburah – 10 Get the stele of revealing itself; set it in thy secret temple – and that temple is already aright disposed – & it shall be your Kiblah for ever. It shall not fade, but miraculous colour shall

come back to it day after day. Close it in locked glass for a proof to the world.

'Secret Temple' is kabbalistically identical to secret house in the previous verse.

Crowley is describing the temple setting used for the invocation of Taphthartharath, the spirit of Mercury.

156 Tipareth – 11 This shall be your only proof. I forbid argument. Conquer! That is enough. I will make easy to you the abstruction from the ill-ordered house in the Victorious City. Thou shalt thyself convey it with worship, o prophet, though thou likest it not. Thou shalt have danger & trouble. Ra-Hoor-Khu is with thee. Worship me with fire & blood; worship me with swords & with spears. Let the woman be girt with a sword before me: let blood flow to my name. Trample down the Heathen; be upon them, o warrior, I will give you of their flesh to eat!

> *156 BABALON. See Liber 418. This number is chiefly important for Part II. It is of no account in the orthodox dogmatic Qabalah. Yet it is 12 × 13, the most spiritual form, 13, of the most perfect number, 12, HVA. (It is TzIVN, Zion, the City of the Pyramids. – ED.)*
>
> *156 BABALON. This most holy and precious name is fully dealt with in Liber 418. Notice 12 × 13 = 156. This was a name given and ratified by Qabalah; 156 is not one of the à priori helpful numbers. It is rather a case of the Qabalah illuminating St John's intentional obscurity.*
>
> *(Liber 777)*

While performing the ritual to Taphthartharath mentioned in the previous verse, link to Cairo, Ra-Hoor-Khuit for a man or the Scarlet Woman.

'Victorious City', Cairo.

157 Netzach – 12 Sacrifice cattle, little and big: after a child.

Aleph is an ox, and Crowley often uses this letter to represent a child = 333. See *The Temple of Solomon the King*. See verse 43.

158 Hod – 13 But not now.

158 refers to eternity.

159 Yesod – 14 Ye shall see that hour, o blessed Beast, and thou the Scarlet Concubine of his desire!

160 Malkuth – 15 Ye shall be sad thereof.
In May 1906, on a train in India, Crowley wrote *The True Greater Ritual of the Pentagram*.
'Sad' = 65 Adonai.

Atu XVI The Tower

161 Kether – 16 Deem not too eagerly to catch the promises; fear not to undergo the curses. Ye, even ye, know not this meaning all.

162 Chokmah – 17 Fear not at all; fear neither men nor Fates, nor gods, nor anything. Money fear not, nor laughter of the folk folly, nor any other power in heaven or upon the earth or under the earth. Nu is your refuge as Hadit your light; and I am the strength, force, vigour, of your arms.
The verse reflects the Martial qualities of Atu XVI.

163 Binah – 18 Mercy let be off; damn them who pity! Kill and torture; spare not; be upon them!
Killing thoughts: 'On the Nature of Silence', *Liber Aleph*.

164 Chesed – 19 That stele they shall call the Abomination of Desolation; count well its name, & it shall be to you as 718.

165 Geburah – 20 Why? Because of the fall of Because, that he is not there again.

> 165 11 × XV should be a number Capricorni Pneumatici. Not yet fulfilled.
>
> *(Liber 777)*

166 Tipareth – 21 Set up my image in the East: thou shalt buy thee an image which I will show thee, especial, not unlike the one thou knowest. And it shall be suddenly easy for thee to do this.

167 Netzach – 22 The other images group around me to support me: let all be worshipped, for they shall cluster to exalt me. I am the visible object of worship; the others are secret; for the Beast & his Bride are they: and for the winners of the Ordeal X. What is this? Thou shalt know.
'Worship' means to unite with, a practical magical technique.

168 Hod – 23 For perfume mix meal & honey & thick leavings of red wine: then oil of Abra-melin and olive oil, and afterward soften & smooth down with rich fresh blood.

Crowley is telling us the importance of the Abra-melin ritual which he was practising almost daily since he purchased Boleskine, which conceivably could also be Ordeal X.

169 – Yesod 24 The best blood is of the moon, monthly: then the fresh blood of a child, or dropping from the host of heaven: then of enemies; then of the priest or of the worshippers: last of some beast, no matter what.

169 is 13 × 13 the numbers of unity and of the lunar High Priestess.

170 – Malkuth 25 This burn: of this make cakes & eat unto me. This hath also another use; let it be laid before me, and kept thick with perfumes of your orison: it shall become full of beetles as it were and creeping things sacred unto me.

Still on the subject of Abra-melin.

XVII The Star

The imagery of the following verses apply particularly to The Emperor ruled by Mars.

171 Kether – 26 These slay, naming your enemies; & they shall fall before you.

Crowley is referring to a scape-goat ritual where the slaughterer names the people before sacrifice. This method is used for friends and foe alike.

172 Chokmah – 27 Also these shall breed lust & power of lust in you at the eating thereof.

The meat of the slaughtered goat is powerful.

173 Binah – 28 Also ye shall be strong in war.

174 Chesed – 29 Moreover, be they long kept, it is better; for they swell with my force. All before me.

175 Geburah – 30 My altar is of open brass work: burn thereon in silver or gold!

Brass is Venus, Silver is Luna, Gold is Sol.

176 Tipareth – 31 There cometh a rich man from the West who shall pour his gold upon thee.
Christian Rozenkreutz.

177 Netzach – 32 From gold forge steel!

178 Hod – 33 Be ready to fly or to smite!

179 Yesod – 34 But your holy place shall be untouched throughout the centuries: though with fire and sword it be burnt down & shattered, yet an invisible house there standeth, and shall stand until the fall of the Great Equinox; when Hrumachis shall arise and the double-wanded one assume my throne and place. Another prophet shall arise, and bring fresh fever from the skies; another woman shall awake the lust & worship of the Snake; another soul of God and beast shall mingle in the globed priest; another sacrifice shall stain the tomb; another king shall reign; and blessing no longer be poured To the Hawk-headed mystical Lord!
'Tomb'. See verse 31 above.

180 Malkuth – 35 The half of the word of Heru-ra-ha, called Hoor-pa-kraat and Ra-Hoor-Khuit.

XVIII The Moon

181 Kether – 36 Then said the prophet unto the God:

182 Chokmah – 37 'I adore thee in the song – I am the Lord of Thebes, and I The inspired forth-speaker of Mentu; For me unveils the veiled sky, The self-slain Ankh-af-na-khonsu Whose words are truth. I invoke, I greet Thy presence, O Ra-Hoor-Khuit! Unity uttermost showed! I adore the might of Thy breath, Supreme and terrible God, Who makest the gods and death To tremble before Thee:- I, I adore thee! 'Appear on the throne of Ra! Open the ways of the Khu! Lighten the ways of the Ka! The ways of the Khabs run through To stir me or still me! Aum! let it fill me!'

183 Binah – 38 So that thy light is in me; & its red flame is as a sword in my hand to push thy order. There is a secret door that I shall make to establish thy way in all the quarters, (these are the adorations, as thou hast written), as it is said: 'The light is mine; its rays consume Me: I have made a secret door Into the House of Ra and Tum, Of Khephra

and of Ahathoor. I am thy Theban, O Mentu, The prophet Ankh-af-na-khonsu! 'By Bes-na-Maut my breast I beat; By wise Ta-Nech I weave my spell. Show thy star-splendour, O Nuit! Bid me within thine House to dwell, O winged snake of light, Hadit! Abide with me, Ra-Hoor-Khuit!'

'Secret door', Atu III. See also the *True Greater Ritual of the Pentagram* and the ritual in *Liber Samekh*.

184 Chesed – 39 All this and a book to say how thou didst come hither and a reproduction of this ink and paper for ever – for in it is the word secret & not only in the English – and thy comment upon this the Book of the Law shall be printed beautifully in red ink and black upon beautiful paper made by hand; and to each man and woman that thou meetest, were it but to dine or to drink at them, it is the Law to give. Then they shall chance to abide in this bliss or no; it is no odds. Do this quickly!

185 Geburah – 40 But the work of the comment? That is easy; and Hadit burning in thy heart shall make swift and secure thy pen.

186 Tipareth – 41 Establish at thy Kaaba a clerk-house: all must be done well and with business way.

Liber Collegii Sancti.

187 Netzach – 42 The ordeals thou shalt oversee thyself, save only the blind ones. Refuse none, but thou shalt know & destroy the traitors. I am Ra-Hoor-Khuit; and I am powerful to protect my servant. Success is thy proof: argue not; convert not; talk not over much! Them that seek to entrap thee, to overthrow thee, them attack without pity or quarter; & destroy them utterly. Swift as a trodden serpent turn and strike! Be thou yet deadlier than he! Drag down their souls to awful torment: laugh at their fear: spit upon them!

See Chapter I, verse 32. 'Traitors', see LIL, *Liber 418*. Also *Liber ף Gnosticorum Missa Minor.*

187 AVPNYM Wheels.

188 Hod – 43 Let the Scarlet Woman beware! If pity and compassion and tenderness visit her heart; if she leave my work to toy with old sweetnesses; then shall my vengeance be known. I will slay me her child: I will alienate her heart: I will cast her out from men: as a shrinking and despised harlot shall she crawl through dusk wet streets, and die cold and an-hungered.

188 PQCh to open.

189 Yesod – 44 But let her raise herself in pride! Let her follow me in my way! Let her work the work of wickedness! Let her kill her heart! Let her be loud and adulterous! Let her be covered with jewels, and rich garments, and let her be shameless before all men!

190 Malkuth – 45 Then will I lift her to pinnacles of power: then will I breed from her a child mightier than all the kings of the earth. I will fill her with joy: with my force shall she see & strike at the worship of Nu: she shall achieve Hadit.

Verses 43–45; see 'The Urn'.

190 the Mystic number of Leo and Teth.

XIX The Sun

191 Kether – 46 I am the warrior Lord of the Forties: the Eighties cower before me, & are abased. I will bring you to victory & joy: I will be at your arms in battle & ye shall delight to slay. Success is your proof; courage is your armour; go on, go on, in my strength; & ye shall turn not back for any!

See Atu VI.

192 Chokmah – 47 This book shall be translated into all tongues: but always with the original in the writing of the Beast; for in the chance shape of the letters and their position to one another: in these are mysteries that no Beast shall divine. Let him not seek to try: but one cometh after him, whence I say not, who shall discover the Key of it all. Then this line drawn is a key: then this circle squared in its failure is a key also. And Abrahadabra. It shall be his child & that strangely. Let him not seek after this; for thereby alone can he fall from it.

Crowley is being cute. DYN is 64, a number of Mercury, and this is the verse of Mercury as Chokmah – see verse 53 below.

193 Binah – 48 Now this mystery of the letters is done, and I want to go on to the holier place.

194 Chesed – 49 I am in a secret fourfold word, the blasphemy against all gods of men.

'Secret fourfold word' TARO.

195 Geburah – 50 Curse them! Curse them! Curse them!

196 Tipareth – 51 With my Hawk's head I peck at the eyes of Jesus as he hangs upon the cross.
See *Liber 888.*

197 Netzach – 52 I flap my wings in the face of Mohammed & blind him.

198 Hod – 53 With my claws I tear out the flesh of the Indian and the Buddhist, Mongol and Din.
A curse from Mercury.

199 Yesod – 54 Bahlasti! Ompehda! I spit on your crapulous creeds.

200 – 55 Let Mary inviolate be torn upon wheels: for her sake let all chaste women be utterly despised among you!

XX Aeon

201 Kether – 56 Also for beauty's sake and love's!

202 Chokmah – 57 Despise also all cowards; professional soldiers who dare not fight, but play; all fools despise!
'Fools'. The secret relationship between 0 and Shin revealed by Eliphas Levi.

> *201 AR, Light (Chaldee). Note 201 = 3 × 67, Binah, as if it were said, 'Light is concealed as a child in the womb of its mother'. The occult retort of the Chaldean Magi to the Hebrew sorcerers who affirmed AVR, Light, 207, is holy enough.*
>
> *(Liber 58)*

203 Binah – 58 But the keen and the proud, the royal and the lofty; ye are brothers!
'Brothers' – The Lovers: or The Brothers Atu VI as Gemini ruled by Mercury.
203 ABR, initials of AB, BN, RVCh, the Trinity. See *Liber 58.*

204 Chesed – 59 As brothers fight ye!
See verse 58. Atu VI.

205 Geburah – 60 There is no law beyond Do what thou wilt.
See *Liber Aleph.*

206 Tipareth – 61 There is an end of the word of the God enthroned in Ra's seat, lightening the girders of the soul.
See *Book of Lies*, 'Chinese Music'.
206 DBR, the Word of Power. A useful acquisition = 'The Gateway of the Word of Light', *Liber 58*.

207 Netzach – 62 To Me do ye reverence! to me come ye through tribulation of ordeal, which is bliss.

> *207 AVR, Light. Contrast with AVB, 9, the astral light, and AVD, 11, the Magical Light. Aub is an illusory thing of witchcraft (cf. Obi, Obeah); Aud is almost = the Kundalini force ('Odic' force). This illustrates well the difference between the sluggish, viscous 9, and the keen, ecstatic 11.*
> *(Liber 58)*

208 Hod **– 63 The fool readeth this Book of the Law, and its comment; & he understandeth it not.**

209 Yesod – 64 Let him come through the first ordeal, & it will be to him as silver.

210 Malkuth – 65 Through the second, gold.
Crowley attributes this and the previous verse to the Paths on the Tree of Life.

XXI The Universe

211 Kether – 66 Through the third, stones of precious water.
Pathworking with reference to Christian Rosenkreuz.

212 Chokmah – 67 Through the fourth, ultimate sparks of the intimate fire.

213 Binah – 68 Yet to all it shall seem beautiful. Its enemies who say not so, are mere liars.

214 Chesed – 69 There is success.
See Chapter 69, the *Book of Lies*.

215 Geburah – 70 I am the Hawk-Headed Lord of Silence & of Strength; my nemyss shrouds the night-blue sky.
A return to topics in Chapter I.

216 Tipareth – 71 Hail! ye twin warriors about the pillars of the world! for your time is nigh at hand.

- Twin is Atu VI
- Pillars, Yachin and Boaz
- World is Atu XXI
- Time is Atu XX

217 Netzach – 72 I am the Lord of the Double Wand of Power; the wand of the Force of Coph Nia – but my left hand is empty, for I have crushed an Universe; & nought remains.

218 Hod – 73 Paste the sheets from right to left and from top to bottom: then behold!

219 Yesod – 74 There is a splendour in my name hidden and glorious, as the sun of midnight is ever the son.

220 Malkuth – 75 The ending of the words is the Word Abrahadabra.

The Book of the Law is Written and Concealed.

Aum. Ha.

220 This is the number of the verses of *Liber Legis*. It represents 10 × 22 (115, i.e. the whole of the Law welded into one). Hence we may be sure that the Law shall stand as it is without a syllable of addition.

1022, the modulus of the Universe of atoms, men, stars. See 'Two New Worlds', *Liber 58*.

Crowley mentions *Two New Worlds* (1907) by 'Fournier d'Albe' in several places – this book abounds with formulae using 1022. The title is evocative – 'Two' is the Dyad or duality, while 'New Worlds' fits in with the New Age. 'The Universe' is the physical universe, which is appropriate for the 4th position. This book would be cutting edge science when published.

PART FOUR

EMERGENT INSPIRATIONS—
ESSAYS AND ANALYSIS

A selection of ideas inspired by and expanded upon
Crowley's writings in Part One of the *Book of Thoth*

CHAPTER THIRTEEN

The Black Brothers

Adeptus (Exemptus)—Completes in perfection all these matters. He then either (a) becomes a Brother of the Left-Hand Path or, (b) is stripped of all his attainments and of himself as well, even of his Holy Guardian Angel, and becomes a babe of the Abyss, who, having transcended the Reason, does nothing but grow in the womb of its mother. It then finds itself a Magister Templi.

(*One Star in Sight*)

Adeptus Exemptus 4° = 7° was attained by Aleister Crowley in 1909. Chesed is below Chokmah and the Abyss. Crossing the Abyss implies dealing with Choronzon discussed in 'The Vision and the Voice'. The Magister Templi pertains to Binah above the Abyss, attained by Crowley in 1910. 'Completes in perfection all these matters': Adeptus Major—Obtains a general mastery of practical Magick, though without comprehension.

When comprehension arises, then comes the choice. On the face of it, becoming a Brother of the Left-Hand Path (i.e. a Black Brother) appears to be an easier option for the ego remains intact as does his magical powers. Retaining one's sense of self and achievement is vital to the Black Brother. For many the Knowledge and Conversation with one's Holy Guardian Angel is the pinnacle of magic, but Crowley makes clear that this is but a step on a long journey—the HGA has to be relinquished for spiritual growth to continue. Choronzon represents the annihilation (fana) of the ego and all its beloved accoutrements which few have the courage ever to do, or accomplish.

The subtle message is that at the level of Adeptus Major, the powers control the magician, and they have no intention of relinquishing that control.

'Transcending reason' reason is a faculty below the Abyss. Above the Abyss all that is uttered is a lie. This is the duality of Atu I described in the *Book of Thoth* and *Liber 333*.

Crossing the Abyss results in rebirth as a babe, described in *LIL*. Crowley's writings thereon are from the perspective of above the Abyss, which is why they remain generally incomprehensible. Crossing the Abyss takes the adept closer to meeting the Hidden Masters.

MacGregor Mathers never even got close to the Abyss, as evidenced by his Golden Dawn teachings; consequently neither did his students. Even assuming Crowley crossed the Abyss, there is precious little evidence that any of his followers achieved it either.

Atu VI, The Lovers, has the alternative title of 'The Brothers'. Lovers implies the union of duality, while Brothers is supposed to be fraternal but all too frequently ends up fratricidal; for example, Cain and Abel.

For brothers, see Chapter 59 of the *Book of Lies*.

The alliteration of Black Brothers reminds us of A∴A∴ which sums to 8, Mercury. Beth is Mercury, doubled is 4, Chesed, known as the accursed Dyad and the number of limitation.

Crowley explicitly links the number 89 to the Black Brothers.

> *A number of sin—restriction. The wrong kind of silence, that of the Black Brothers.*

Chapter 89, 'Unprofessional Conduct' of the *Book of Lies* expands on this.

> *Frater P. had been annoyed by a scurvy doctor, the number of whose house was 89.*
>
> *He shows that his mind was completely poisoned in respect of that number by his allowing himself to be annoyed.*
>
> *(But note that a good Qabalist cannot err. 'In Him all is right'.*
> *89 is body—that which annoys—and the Angel of the Lord of Despair*

and Cruelty. Also 'Silence' and 'Shut Up'. The four meanings completely describe the chapter.)

The tarot card referred to is the 9 of Swords, Cruelty.

Crowley gives vivid descriptions of the Black Brothers. He sums up the 12th Aethyr LOE as:

The Second Mystery: the cup-bearer of Babalon the beautiful. The Holy Grail manifested to the M.T., with the first knowledge of the Black Brothers.

In other words, it was his spiritual progress that revealed the existence of the Black Brothers. Progress on the Path requires overcoming opposition:

But if this be satisfactorily accomplished, and the spirit be yet disobedient, the implication is that some hostile force is at work to hinder the operation. It will then become advisable to discover the nature of that force, and to attack and destroy it. This makes the ceremony more useful than ever to the Magician, who may thereby be led to unveil a black magical gang whose existence he had not hitherto suspected.

His need to check the vampiring of a lady in Paris by a sorceress once led FRATER PERDURABO to the discovery of a very powerful body of black magicians, which whom he was obliged to war for nearly 10 years before their ruin was complete and irremediable as it now is.

(Book IV, Part 3, Chapter 16)

The Single Supreme Ritual is the attainment of the Knowledge and Conversation of the Holy Guardian Angel. *It is the raising of the complete man in a vertical straight line.*

Any deviation from this line tends to become black magic. Any other operation is black magic.

(Book IV, Part 3, Chapter 21)

There is a modern obsession with calling up demons, which Crowley deals with:

It is, however, always easy to call up the demons, for they are always calling you; and you have only to step down to their level and fraternize with them. They will tear you in pieces at their leisure. Not at once;

they will wait until you have wholly broken the link between you and
your Holy Guardian Angel before they pounce, lest at the last moment
you escape.

Anthony of Padua and (in our own times) 'Macgregor' Mathers are
examples of such victims.

(*Book VI*, Part 3, Chapter 21)

There is a sound reason for calling demons.

Nevertheless, every magician must firmly extend his empire to the depth
of hell. 'My adepts stand upright, their heads above the heavens, their feet
below the hells'.

(*Book VI*, Part 3, Chapter 21)

AL II.5 alludes to the above

Behold! the rituals of the old time are black. Let the evil ones be cast away; let
the good ones be purged by the prophet! Then shall this Knowledge go aright.

As a consequence, Crowley says this:

To mock at Hadit is therefore evidently very much what is meant by the
mysterious phrase in the 'New Testament' with regard to the Unpardon-
able Sin, the 'blasphemy against the Holy Ghost'. A star forsaken by Hadit
would thus be in the condition of real death it is this state which is charac-
teristic of the 'Black Brothers', as they are described in other parts of this
Comment, and elsewhere in the Holy Books of the A∴A∴.

(Commentary to *AL*, II.56)

Black Brothers are magicians who fail to cross the Abyss, exemplified by Choronzon.

Beware, o my Son, lest thou cling overmuch to this Mode of Magick; for
it is lesser than that Other, and if thou neglect That Other, then is thy
Danger fearful and imminent, for it is the Edge of the Abyss of Choronzon,
where are the lonely Towers of the Black Brothers. Also the Formulation
of the Object in the Eagle is by a Species of Intoxication, so that His Nature
is of Dream or Delirium, and thus there may be Illusion.

(De Aquilae Sumenda)

Black Brothers have only consideration for themselves.

Such are the Black Brothers, that cry: I am I, they that deny Love,
restricting it to their own Nature.

(*De Dracone, Quae Est Aquila*, Serpens, Scorpion)

See Chapter 89 in the *Book of Lies*, above.

'I am I' is the selfish nature of the Black Brothers.
    O my Son, know this concerning the Black Brothers, that cry: I am I.
This is Falsity and Delusion, for the Law endureth not Exception. So then
these Brethren are not apart, as they vainly think being wrought by Error;
but are peculiar Combinations of Nature in Her Variety.

(De Fratribus Nigris)

The Black Brother resist change.

Of the Black Brothers, o my Son, will I write these Things following.
I have told thee already concerning Change, how it is the Law, because
every Change is an Act of Love under will. So then He that is Adept
Exempt, whether in our Holy Order or another, may not remain in the
Pillar of Mercy, because it is not balanced, but is unstable. Therefore is the
Choice given unto him, whether he will destroy his Temple, and give up
his Life, extending it to Universal Life, or whether he will make a Fortress
about that Temple, and abide therein, in the false Sphere of Daath, which
is in the Abyss. And to the Adepts of our Holy Order this Choice is ter-
rible; by Cause that they must abandon even Him whose Knowledge and
Conversation they have attained. Yet, o my Son, they have much Help of
our Order in this Aeon, because the general Formula is Love, so that their
habit itself urges them to the Bed of our Lady BABALON. Know then the
Black Brothers by this true Sign of their Initiation of iniquity, that that
they resist Change, restrict and deny Love, fear Death. Percutiantur.

(De Fratribus Nigris Filiis Iniquitatis)

'Fear Death' is particularly interesting, for Death is the codeword for
Initiation, as in 'die daily'.

Now, o my Son, having understood the heaven that is within thee, accord-
ing to thy will, learn this concerning the hell of the slaves of the slave-gods,

that it is a true place of torment. For they, restricting themselves, and being divided in will, are indeed the servants of sin, and they suffer, because, not being united in love with the whole Universe, they perceive not beauty, but ugliness and deformity, and, not being united in understanding thereof. Conceive only of darkness and confusion, beholding evil therein. Thus at last they come, as did the Manichaeans, to find, to their terror, a division even in the one, not that division which we know for the craft of love, but a division of hate. And this, multiplying itself, conflict upon conflict, endeth in hotchpot, and in the impotence and envy of Choronzon, and in the abominations of the abyss. And of such the Lords are the Black Brothers, who seek by their sorceries to confirm themselves in division, yet in this even is no true evil, for love conquereth all, and their corruption and disintegration is also the victory of Babalon.

(De Inferno Servorum)

Atu XI and Babalon is germane to the Black Brothers.

But now let me show how this Lion of Courage is more especially the Light in thee, as Leo is the House of the Sun that is the Father of Light. And it is thus: that thy Light, conscious of itself, is the Source and Instigator of thy Will, enforcing it to spring forth and conquer. Therefore also is his Nature strong with hardihood and Lust of Battle, else shouldst thou fear that which is unlike thee, and avoid it, so that thy Separateness should increase upon thee. For this Cause he that is defective in Courage becometh a Black Brother, and To Dare is the Crown of all thy Virtue, the Root of the Tree of Magick.

(De Leone)

The silence of the Black Brothers is contrasted with the silence of The Fool. Clearly Babalon is Key to defeating them.

The Nature of this Silence is shewn also by the God Harpocrates, the Babe in the Lotus, who is also the Serpent and the Egg, that is, the Holy Ghost. This is the most secret of all Energies, the Seed of all being, and therefore must He be sealed up in an Ark from the Malice of the Devourers. If then by thine Art thou canst conceal thyself in thine own Nature, this is Silence, this, and not Nullity of Consciousness else were a Stone more perfect in Adeptship that thou. But, abiding in thy Silence, thou art in a City of Refuge, and the Waters prevail not against the Lotus that enfoldeth thee. This Ark or Lotus is then the Body of OUR LADY BABALON, without

which thou were the Prey of Nile and of the Crocodiles that are therein.
Now, o my Son, mark thou well this that I will write for thine Advertise-
ment and Behoof, that this Silence, though it be Perfection of Delight,
is but the Gestation of thy Lion, and in thy Season thou must dare, and
come forth to the Battle. Else, were not this Practice of Silence akin to the
Formula of Separateness of the Black Brothers?

(De Natura Silentii Nostri)

The Cult of the Slave-Gods is the work of the Black Brothers and requires
a call to action.

Know that the Cult of the Slave-Gods is a Device of those Black Broth-
ers. All that stagnateth is thereof, and thence cometh not Stability, but
Putrefaction. Endure not thou the static Standards either in Thought or
in Action Resist not even the Change that is the Rottenness of Choronzon,
but rather speed it, so that the elements may combine by Love under Will.
Since the Black Brothers and their Cults set themselves against Change,
do thou break them asunder. Yea, though of bad come worse, continue in
that Way; for it is as if thou didst open an Abscess, the first Effect being
noisome exceedingly, but the last Cleanness. Heed not then, whoso crieth
Anarchy, and Immorality, and Heresy against thee, and feareth to destroy
Abuse lest worse Things come of it. For the Will of the Universe in its
Wholeness is to Truth, and thou dost well to purge it from its Constive-
ness. For it is written that there is no bond that can unite the Divided by
Love, so that only those Complexes which are in Truth Simplicities, being
built Cell by Cell unto an Unity by Virtue of Love under Will, are worthy
to endure in their Progression.

(De Virtute Chirurgica)

Because

There is great danger in me; for who doth not understand these runes shall
make a great miss. He shall fall down into the pit called Because, and there
he shall perish with the dogs of Reason.

(*Liber AL*, II.27)

Some technical aspects of this verse had better be mentioned. First
of all, HADIT equals 29 by the Qabalah, and so does BECAUSE.
(HADIT = 5 + 1 + 4 + 10 + 9 = 29).

BECAUSE = 2 + 5 + 3 + 1 + 6 + 7 + 5 = 29. 'Because' means, therefore, a false sense of personal identity that may be taken for the true one,
Hadit, by the unwary. Since the word 'Because' is evidently connected
with the process of reasoning, we may equate it with the undisciplined
Ruach, or Ego. In this sense 'pit' may not mean the Abyss, but a trap.

(Liber AL, II.27, commentary)

Crowley relates 'Reason' to the functions of the chakras and to
Choronzon.

REASON = 200 + 5 + 1 + 7 + 70 + 50 = 333, the number of Choronzon,
'dispersion'. (See Liber 418, the tenth Aethyr.) 'Dogs of Reason' are, therefore, the 'Black Brothers'. Why shall he perish with the 'Black Brothers'?
Because he will join their current. It manifests itself in the lower cakkrams,
particularly those of the heart and the navel. The bodily Prana is deflected
by it. Man's vital force should rise from the Muladhara Cakkram to the
higher head centres, Visudhi, Ajna and Sahashara (See Liber V.); instead,
it disperses itself in a reflex, confused, undirected activity of the intermedi-
ary centres. In the trained Initiate, the lower Cakkrams function entirely
under the control of the head centres. Initiates are therefore frequently
considered by 'mediums' and 'Clairvoyants' to be 'cold', or 'Pitiless', or
'without compassion'. Imperfect seers call the Initiate's aura 'black', being
unable to perceive the radiation of the higher centres (See AL I, 16–18, 21,
27, 28, 29, 60; II, 6, 14, 23, 50–53; III, 19–20, 22, 38, 44–45, 49, 74, 75.)
The 'Black Brothers', on the other hand, seem to them to 'radiate sunlight'.
The Prana in them never rises to the higher centres at all, and its rate of
vibration is low enough to be 'seen of the unseeing'. The only radiation of
their higher centres is the normal nerve circuitry of the body. (The Cakkrams, if developed and functioning, are like electric transformers. They
step up the vibratory rate of Prana. The faster they spin, the 'fainter': and
'faerier' becomes the Initiate's aura, until it becomes attuned tot he Aura
of the Milky Way—the 'Orgone light' of Wilhelm Reich—the 'kisses of the
stars'. Or, if you prefer, to the Body of Nuit, which of course is omnipres-
ent. Any lower forms of energy exist in it.)

(Liber AL, II.27, commentary)

If the Aspirant becomes attuned to 'Because' he may mistake the 'Dog
Syndrome' of Cakkram malfunction for the 'God Syndrome' of higher

Cakkram awakening. He will identify himself with the Egoic Complex of the 'Black Brethren'.

(*Liber AL*, II.27, commentary)

'We have nothing with the outcast and the unfit'. Nothing—Nuit, Outcast—Initiates who have been expelled for wrong-doing, that is, 'Black Brethren'. Unfit—those as yet incapable of being initiated, that is, the great majority of mankind. We have Nuit in common with them. To the 'Black Brethren' She manifests Herself as 333—that Influence that will eventually destroy them, that is, force them to cross the Abyss whether they 'will' or no.

(*Liber AL*, II.21, commentary)

Dogs of reason

Yet will I not fall into the Pit called Because, there to perish with the dogs of reason. There is no reason in me; I seek Understanding, O Mother of Heaven.

(Hymns to the Star Goddess, Frater Achad)

The meaning of the verse is then that this spilth of the orgia of the Knowledge and Conversation of the Holy Guardian Angel becomes the nourishment and the means of intoxication of the dogs, i.e. of animals of a lower stage of evolution. It is however, hinted that they contain in themselves the hidden godhead. See CCXX II:19. They have only to reverse their magical formula to attain the divinity. Note also the use of the word 'lap' which suggests their thirst, eagerness and enjoyment, but also is connected with the symbolism of the number 111. This implies the 'thick darkness' and the 'sudden death' involved in the process of Initiation. There is also the whole doctrine of 'The Fool'. Besides all this, the word 'lap' is in the Angelic Language. (See The Equinox 8, The 48 Calls or Keys) Because thus indicating that the limitation and sorrow of these dogs is due to their subservience to the faculty of reason. There is great danger in me; for who doth not understand these runes shall make a great miss. He shall fall down into the pit called Because, and there he shall perish with the dogs of Reason. Now a curse upon Because and his kin! May Because be accursed for ever! If Will stops and cries Why, invoking Because, then Will stops and does nought. If Power asks why, then is Power weakness. Also reason is a lie; for there is

a factor infinite and unknown; and all their words are skew-wise. Enough
of Because! Be he damned for a dog! (Liber CCXX II:27–33.)

(*Liber 65*, Chapter 4, verse 60 commentary)

Enough of Because! Be he damned for a dog!

(*AL*, II.33)

The word 'dog' has occurred before this. Firstly, the dog is used as a symbol
of a form which would restrict a God who indwelt it. Again 'There is death
for the dogs', that is, to restrict free action ends in stopping it once and
for all. Further 'the dogs of Reason'. The thought of the mind born of and
nourished by the senses tends to restrict the self, to impose the will of the
world upon it, whereas the use of the world is to provide it with objects of
love through which it can fulfil itself and know itself. To become passive
towards the thoughts and the senses is to accept the fetters of a slave.

(Djeridensis Comment on *AL*, II.33)

Powers of the Black Brothers

There is a Siddha in Yoga, described by Patanjali, which consists of the abil-
ity to penetrate another's mind, 'and assume control thereof'. This 'power'
is often employed by 'Black Brothers', especially if the other mind belongs to
one of the sick currents started by themselves. In such a case, the cakkrams
of the owner of the mind are attuned to the influence of the 'Black Brother',
and his or her astral is 'in sympathy' with the 'Black Brother' influence.

This unworthy 'power' is never used by true Gods. The Perfect crossed
the Abyss: He is defined as being at least a Master of the temple. True
Initiates NEVER interfere with another human's will. However, they are
in communion with ALL human wills in a manner incomprehensible by,
and inexplicable to, the profane. Even the highest types of Samadhi give
only a pale idea of this communion. It is the true and genuine Communion
of the Saints, and the Grail, the Cup in the hand of our Lady BABALON,
is its symbol.

(Commentary to *AL*, I.45)

(By 'displease another star' is not meant to offend the prejudices of its
personality! He or she who is doing his or her True Will knows when he
or she really diseases another. AS to destroy or deform: the influence of the
'Black Brothers' is towards this, they being insane, and their egos hostile

to other Beings. You must learn to detect it. Also, you must not mistake the destruction of a person who is interfering with your True Will—such as a 'Black Brother'!—with the attempt to destroy—it can never be more than an attempt—or deform that person's Starry Nature. See Liber NV, verses 9–11. The key is that the influence of the 'Black Brothers' is turned against any personality that is expressing, or trying to express, its Starry Nature. Their diseased egos feel this, rightly, as an attack on their integrity. They rear love, because love will destroy—that is, change—them.) Mutual consent to the act is the condition thereof. It must, of course, be understood that such consent is not always explicit. There are cases when seduction or rape may be emancipation or initiation to another. Such acts can only be judged by their results.

(Commentary on *AL*, I.52)

Religion, as understood by the vile Puritan, is the very opposite of all this. He—it—seems to wish to kill his—its—soul by forbidding every expression of it, and every practice which might awaken it to expression. (True. For the awakening of the soul means change, under which the present form and condition of the ego must 'die'. Fearing this death, they confirm themselves in stagnation and resist change. This is no effect of the telepathic 'radiation' of the 'Black Brothers'.) To hell with this Verbotenism!

(Commentary on *AL*, I.63)

Delusions of the Black Brothers

'Come unto me' is a 'foolish word'—see our Commentary to AL I, 11—is a direct condemnation of 'Black Brotherhood', that is, Imperfect Initiation. The 'Black Brother' opens his arms to his fellow men and cries out, 'Come unto me, ye who suffer, and be consoled!' He does this by the unbalance of his Ego. He has received a sufficient influx of Magick Force to 'feel good', and his spiritual pride infuses him with pity for his fellow beings, particularly his own species. He wants to 'console' them. In point of fact, however, he will enslave them, for he is unable to see their true nature at all. If could see it, he would understand what Hadit means by stating categorically: 'it is I that go'.

(Commentary *AL*, II.27)

In the view of Crowley, MacGregor Mathers downfall came about through an imperfect initiation.

Separation from the Black Brothers

The innkeeper is the Guardian of the Mysteries, and the king the Authority by which men's lives are governed. It is his business to protect the guests from the arrogance of the Black Brothers, but also to prevent their malice from making the sacrament unlawful.

(Commentary to *Liber 65*, Chapter 4, Verse 14)

We are twice told that he 'stood' which is to be contrasted with the activity of 'going' of the Holy Guardian Angel. It is the peculiar token of any God that he should go. For this reason he bears the Ankh or sandal-strap in the Egyptian monuments. This antithesis is connected with the conception of the Black Brothers as shutting themselves up, or resenting change.

(Commentary to *Liber 65*, Chapter 4, Verse 34)

However, it is not as easy to separate a Black Brother as one might think.

... i.e. he has acquiesced in duality, established an interior conflict in himself, and ceremonially blasphemed and denied the unity of his own True Will. Appalling as is such a catastrophe, it lacks the element of finality since the principles involved do not extend above Tiphereth. He has become a Black Magician no doubt, but this is far indeed from being a Black Brother. It cannot even be said that such an one thereby manifests any tendency to become a Black Brother when the time is ripe; for his union even with the personification of Evil is also an act of love under will, though that will be false and vitiated by every conceivable defect and error. His chief danger is presumably that the intensity of the suffering which results from this may, as in the case of Glyndon in Zanoni, lead him to seek to escape altogether from Magick, to refrain from any act of love for fear lest he stray still farther from his true path.

(Commentary to *Liber 65*, Chapter 4, Verse 34)

Crowley again feels the need to define the Black Brothers.

The Universe is a constant flux. To desire repose is thus contrary to Nature herself. We accept this fact and define the Black Brothers directly as those who seek to check the course of events. The bourgeois is for us therefore a clumsy ignorant amateur Black Magician.

(Commentary to *Liber 65*, Chapter 4, Verse 61)

The complexities of understanding the Black Brothers are demonstrated in this quote from the 6th Aethyr MAZ—crossing the Abyss into Binah is no guarantee.

> For the Black Brothers lift not up their heads thus far into the Holy Chokmah, for they were all drowned in the great flood, which is Binah, before the true vine could be planted upon the holy hill of Zion.
>
> Accepting annihilation, instantly destroys the myriad of insane images which hastened to occupy the vacuum created by the leap of the Exempt Adept into the Abyss. Had he faltered, he would have become—against his will—a 'Black Brother'. But this being involuntary, he would not have attempted to maintain his coherence, as the Black Brothers do. He would therefore, have been destroyed at once; that is, to outward appearance he would have become a demented babbler.

(18th Aethyr ZEN)

The Black Brothers in Moonchild

Moonchild is an account Crowley's experience of battling with the Black Brothers.

> Balloch contemptuously released his victim—who was a brave enough man in an ordinary way, and would have had the blood of his own Sultan, though he knew that the guards would cut him to pieces within the next ten seconds, for the least of such words as had been addressed to him. But Balloch was his Superior in the Black Lodge, which rules by terror and by torture; its first principle was to enslave its members. The bully Balloch became a whimpering cur at the slightest glance of the dreaded S.R.M.D.

Balloch is William Berridge while S.R.M.D. is MacGregor Mathers.

> Two days before the beginning of the operation, a telegram from Paris reached him. It stated that, as he suspected, Balloch and Douglas were the forces behind the attack; further, that Grey's presence in Naples was known, and that three members of the Black Lodge had left Paris for Italy.

Mather's power base was in Paris. The identity of Douglas is not clear but see Chapter 11.

The Black Brothers in the Book of Thoth

Apart from the history of how the Golden Dawn was formed (pages 7 and 8) by Mathers and Frau Sprengel, the Black Lodge is mentioned in the commentary on the Prince of Disks and Atu XIII.

CHAPTER FOURTEEN

The gematria of Aleister Crowley

A selection of numbers relating to Aleister Crowley's system of gematria which express creativity and spirituality.

The importance of eight

Eight on its side is the symbol of infinity—see 2 of Disks:

> *... production is equal to destruction in the movement which conserves life; and there is no point in infinity which cannot be the centre of a circle whose circumference expands and indefinitely recedes into space.*
>
> (Levi, *Mysteries of Magic*)

Crowley ascribes 120 as a development from finity to infinity:

> *SMK, Samech, a prop. Also MVSDI, basis, foundation. 120 = 1 × 2 × 3 × 4 × 5, and is thus a synthesis of the power of the pentagram. (Also 1 + 2 + ... + 15 = 120.) Hence its importance in the 5 = 6 ritual, q.v. supra Equinox III. I however disagree in part; it seems to me to symbolise a lesser redemption than that associated with Tiphereth. Compare at least the numbers 0.12 and 210 in Liber Legis and Liber 418, and extol their superiority.*

For while the first is the sublime formula of the infinite surging into fin-
ity, and the latter the supreme rolling-up of finity into infinity, the 120
can symbolise at the best a sort of intermediate condition of stability. For
how can one proceed from the 2 to the 0? 120 is also ON, a very important
name of God.

See *AL*, I.4, *AL*, I.28, *AL*, I.29, *AL*, I.32, *AL*, I.46, *AL*, I.47, *AL*, I.51,
AL, II.21, *AL*, II. 32.

8

Cheth is the 8th Letter; = 418 a number of ABRAHADABRA; and of
Atu VII.

The Ogdoad, Intellect (also Change in Stability). Derived from 2 and 3 by
multiplication, 8 = 2 cubed.

Change in Stability is the 2 of Disks. The Coptic H is 8. On the Tree of
Life 8 is Hod and Mercury. A∴A∴ is 8. ABH to will, AHB to love (Love
is the law, love under will), DAG a fish.

80

The number of ם, the 'lightning-struck Tower' of the Tarot. 8 = Intellect,
Mercury; its most material form is Ruin, as Intellect in the end is divided
against itself.

See *AL* I.47 commentary.
   80 is the number of Yesod, the 9th Sephiroth, the Universe and KS
throne (indicating the Path from Yesod to Binah). VOD union, assem-
bling, MM water.

88

11 × 8 ChNKY, initiation into the Mysteries, a fiery number.

800

The letter Peh in its final form.

QShTh, the Rainbow. The Promise of Redemption (8)—8 as Mercury, Intellect, the Ruach, Microprosopus, the Redeeming Son—in its most material form.

(*Liber Samekh*, 'The Preliminary Invocation of the Goetia')

888

Jesus (Greek numeration):

The grand scale of 8. In Greek numeration therefore IHΣΟΎΣ the Redeemer, connecting with 6 because of its 6 letters. This links Greek and Hebrew symbolism; but remember that the mystic Iesous and Yeheshua have no more to do with the legendary Jesus of the Synoptics and the Methodists than the mystic IHVH has to do with the false God who commanded the murder of innocent children. The 13 of the Sun and the Zodiac was perhaps responsible for Buddha and his 12 disciples, Christ and his 12 disciples, Charlemagne and his 12 peers, &c., &c., but to disbelieve in Christ or Charlemagne is not to alter the number of the signs of the Zodiac. Veneration for 666 does not commit me to admiration for Napoleon and Gladstone.

48

KVKB Mercury, ChYL a woman, strength, an army.

Magic square of Mercury

64

8 × 8 DIN and DNI, Intelligences (the twins) of Mercury. Liber Israfel, prophecy, golden waters, Noah, sphere of Venus. The number of squares on a chess board.

260

Tiriel, Intelligence of Mercury, exalted, The Concealed, gather, draw together.

2080

Thaphthartharath Spirit of Mercury.

256

Eighth power of 2. Light, an Urn. Aaron.

512

Ninth power of 2.

Beth

Beth is associated with Mercury; Beth is 2 which is also Chokmah and the Grade of Magus. See Liber 73.

Eight-lettered name

- Octinomos
- RPSTOVAL
- Baphomet
- Cauldron
- IAHDONHI = YHVH + ADNY 26 + 65 = 91 (*Book of Lies*)

'8 colour plates'

Correspond to the Eight Princes of Abra-melin:

- Amaimon
- Ariton
- Asmodee
- Astaroth
- Belzebud
- Magot
- Oriens
- Paimon

Symbols

- Caduceus
- Winged Egg
- Winged Globe

Astrology

Mercury rules Gemini and Virgo (where it is also exalted) Atu 6 and Atu 9.

Books

- *Book of Thoth*
- *Book of Lies* (lying is a characteristic of Mercury)
- *Liber 2*

Ritual

Abra-melin, Bornless Ritual, Unborn Ritual, Liber Israfel, Goetic Ritual.

ThROA

'The Theory of the Correspondences of the Tarot' largely addresses gematria, the science of numbers starting with 13, the number of AChD, unity, and AHBH, love. Add the two numbers together for another important number, 26, YHVH the four lettered Name of God.

Crowley then switches to another four lettered word, TARO, which is the preferred spelling. This word is permuted into the famous:

> TARO—Tarot ROTA—Wheel TORA—The Law (ie Torah) ATOR—The Goddess Ahathoor

Crowley suggests TARO can be read as 0 = 2: 'The Universe—the new-born Sun—Zero'. The sum of ThROA is 671 = 11 × 61, the Gate or Door, the letter Daleth and the Empress. 61 is AIN, Nothing or Zero, while 11 is 'the number of Magical Expansion' which is not explained.

The number 671 has very interesting mathematical properties. 6 + 7 + 1 = 14, the number of the Empress (Hathor); 6 − 7 + 1 = 0 taking us back to zero. On the Kabbalistic Tree of Life the Path from Zero to the other numbers is tricky, but here it is implicit in the mathematics, for the symbol of Venus links all ten Sephiroth on the Tree of Life.

671 links all Crowley's favourite topics—the Tarot, the Wheel ('Wheel and Whoa!'), The Law (*Liber AL*), and the Goddess Babalon, while Liber 671 is Crowley's interpretation of the Neophyte Ceremony.

671 is the number of ADNY, the Lord, spelt in full which gives the masculine balance. Another four lettered name, ADNY, is 65, the constant for the Magic Square of Mars, and the number of the palaces. Liber 65 written by Crowley has five sections corresponding to the five elements; 65 multiplied by 4 is 260, the magical constant of the Magic Square of Mercury.

6 + 1 and 7 (77) = 7 × 11. Add Zero (The Fool) to 77 we get 78; 77 is the link to the Supreme System of Magick, for in the Magic Square of 11 each column and row adds up to 671.

While Crowley plays with the 6 and 1, he omits the 7 for good reason, for it leads directly to this powerful magical system.

Seven is obviously the number of the planets and the 'Days of the Week', and it is the number of Venus. A pattern is forming.

Returning to *Book T*, the Minor Arcana, are listed in decanate order starting with the 5 of Wands in Leo. These cards are grouped into planetary rulerships starting with Saturn in the Chaldean Order. He also orders the cards according to the 'Days of the Week' which emphasises the importance of the number 7. The diagram of the 'Days of the Week' on page 11 of *Book of Thoth* is another of Crowley's hints to the system.

The Opening of the Key does not have a spread for the planets! Such a spread is easy to construct—simply deal out the cards into seven stacks in a circle and place the final card in the centre. This spread is perfect, for it has none of the defects of the other stages. Each stack has 11 cards, the first stack is Saturn, the second is Jupiter, and so on. The final card is the Significator, which has a powerful function not to be confused with the general meaning as known by tarot students.

Mathematics drives the system, and mathematics drives the powerful hidden OOTK system. YHVH, ADNY, and TARO are in essence interchangeable. BABALON is the seven-lettered name of the Goddess; what is the 11-lettered name? ABRAHADABRA, another of Crowley's favourite names, is 418, the sum of a series of numbers from 13 to 31 and the sum is also 13. 418 is the number of Cheth, The Chariot.

Add one to 418, and we have 419, the number of Teth and the Lust card. In his commentary on this card Crowley includes Waratah-Blossom, dedicated to Babalon.

Number clusters

Clusters of numbers reveal important details. One such is found centred on 78. The number either side carries the same characteristics as the
central number also known as a colel.

76

A secret or refuge mentioned in the commentary to *LIL* (70 is 7 Venus),
which permeates all things; 76 is also KVN, a cake offering. The commentary to the 76th verse of *Liber 220* questions whether Crowley was
prepared to progress. The character of this number is intense fire and
of the Sun (the *Book of Lies*). Seeing through the glamour cast by Maya.

77

The number 77 is at the centre of the Ace of Disks in the Sigillum
Sanctum of the Order of A∴A∴ and the chapter of the same number in
the *Book of Lies*:

> *77 OZ THE SUBLIME AND SUPREME SEPTENARY IN ITS*
> *MATURE MAGICAL MANIFESTATION THROUGH MATTER—AS*
> *IT IS WRITTEN—AN HE-GOAT ALSO.*

OZ is a Goat (Atu XV), the intense direction of prayer and study of
gematria, and LAYLAH which occupies much of the discourse of the
Book of Lies; 77 is MGDL, towers or citadels (Enochian magic), and MZL
the secret influence from Kether which manifests as Atu I. The most
propitious time is of the night, Laylah, and the Ikhlas prayer of Islam.
The experience of which is to cause trembling and flow (kundalini).
GOD and DOG are both 77:

> *Is a God to live in a dog? No! but the highest are of us. They shall rejoice,*
> *our chosen: who sorroweth is not of us.*
>
> (*Liber AL*, II.19)

God and Dog represent dualism, a polarity. If the O is zero, then we
have GD good fortune, and DG a fish (i.e. Christ). The importance of 7 is

evident everywhere in Crowley's writings. Furthermore, God and Dog point to Sirius or Sothis, wherein lies a mystery.

78

> *Most venerable because MZLA is shown as the influence descending from On High, whose key is the Tarot: and we possess the Tarot. The proper number of the name of the Messenger of the Most Exalted One.*
>
> *MZLA, the influence from Kether. The number of the cards of the Tarot, and of the 13 paths of the Beard of Macroprosopus. Note 78 = 13 × 6. Also AIVAS, the messenger.*
>
> (Aleister Crowley, *The Equinox 5: The Temple of Solomon the King*)

Half 78 is 39:

> *YHVH AChD 'Tetragrammaton is One', although He is composed of 4 letters, hence the triumph over the power of 4, limitation. But this explanation is not as clear, satisfactory and convincing with that singular feeling of ecstatic illumination which one rightly demands of the Qabalistic demonstration. There should be some further gematria of 39 not yet discovered. 2 is Beth, Atu I, Mayan the Great Sorcerer. 78 = Mezla MZLA the Influence from Kether, and the number of the Tarot Cards. I.e. she destroys him by his own energies.*
>
> (*Liber 418*, 2nd Aethyr)

DLH is to draw forth, bring out, or reveal; GVL to rejoice; ZBL, to dwell in.

78 is 13 × 6, AChD unity or Atu II The Moon and The Sun (Tipareth) conjoined; it is also the number of Abuldiz and Aiwass, and the chapter 'Wheel and Woah' which appears in the *Book of Thoth*. AVMAL is an angel of the 10 of Wands.

Revelation often appears in a dream ChLM, a source of initiation ChNK (Enoch), sustained by bread LChM and salt MLCh. See 'Wheel and Whoa!'

79

The number of Yachin and Boaz, the two Pillars of Mercy and Severity in the Temple. After the exertions on the Path (78), times of recuperation and rest are required (Chapter 79 of the *Book of Wisdom and Folly*).

Between the two Pillars is a conjunction or union (ODH) and liberation (MLT). See the 2 of Disks, Change.

This number is omitted from the list of Prime Numbers in 777.

80

The number of Peh and Atu XVI, The House of God, as 8 Hod, Mercury and a mouth. It is also the number of YSVD Yesod, the 9th Sephirah which is a secret SVDY-YH ADNY is its God. There has to be the Lord, Adonai somewhere. KS a throne links this number back to Binah. The element is water MM. *AL* I.47 is key:

> 61 = {Aleph-Vau-Nun}. But the True Nothing of Nuit is 8, 80, 418. Now 8 is {Cheth}, which spelt fully is 418—{Cheth-Yod-Tau}. And 418 is ABRAHADABRA, the word of Ra-Hoor-Khuit. Now 80 is {Pe}, the letter of Ra-Hoor-Khuit. (Qy. this?) (Could 80 = {infinity} 0. Infinity × Zero?)
>
> (Appendix to Liber 220)

81

The number of Yesod and the square of the moon, also KSA throne, and the first day of the full moon. Perhaps more importantly this is the number of IAO.

> For I am perfect, being Not; and my number is nine by the fools; but with the just I am eight, and one in eight: Which is vital, for I am none indeed. The Empress and the King are not of me; for there is a further secret.
>
> (AL, II.15)

This sequence of numbers could be expanded further, but for now they indicate the Sephiroth 7, 8, and 9.

64

The sum of the number is 10, influence from another quarter, i.e. the Formula of the Tetragrammaton, while this number is the sum of 8 squared.

The comment to *AL*, I.64 is 'The supreme affirmation'.

The number of squares on a chess board, the perfect game of logic and strategy—see Richard Réti on page 22, and expanded in *Liber Aleph*, 'De Ratione Magi Vitae':

> *Study Logic, which is the Code of the Laws of Thought. Study the Method of Science, which is the Application of Logic to the Facts of the Universe. Think not that thou canst ever abrogate these Laws, for though they be Limitations, they are the rules of thy Game which thou dost play. For in thy Trances though thou becomest That which is not subject to those Laws, they are still final in respect of these Things which thou hast set them to govern. Nay, o my son, I like not this Word, govern, for a Law is but a Statement of the nature of the Thing to which it applieth. Nor nothing is compelled save only by Nature of its own true Will. So therefore human Law is a Statement of the Will and of the Nature of Man, or else it is a Falsity contrary thereunto, and becometh null and of no Effect.*

Therein is contained another a formula, samadhi on random thoughts in a trance become organised.

The Book of Lies, Chapter 64

> *I was discussing oysters with a crony: God sent to me the angels DIN and DONI.*

For oysters—see Chapter 3 on the High Priestess. DYN and DNY are the twin Mercurial Intelligences in Gemini. KKB YChD is 'A shining glittering sphere which unites into one'. *Liber Israfel* is numbered 64. NBVAH is prophecy, ANHH is a deep sigh, i.e. breath. NVGH is the sphere of Venus, NVCh is Noah, MY ZHB is the golden waters (influence from Tipareth). Add 1 to 64 is ADNY, the Lord 65.

65 the number of Abra-Melin servitors of magot and kore

Crowley's commentary on *AL* I.1:

> *Nu being 56 and Had 9, their conjunction results in 65, Adonai, the Holy Guardian Angel. Also Hoor, who combines the force of the Sun with that of Mars. Adonai is primarily Solar, but 65 is a number sacred to Mars.*

See the Sepher Sephiroth, and 'The Wake World' in *Knox Om Pax* for further details on 65.

> *Note moreover, the sixty-five pages of the MS. of Liber Legis. Or, counting NV 56, Had 10, we get 66, which is (1–11). Had is further the centre of the Key Word ABRAHADABRA.*

AVChYM is weasels and other terrible animals. ChZN is 'defective'. Crowley makes the point that MacGregor Mathers is ruled by Mars, and that mistakes were made in his initiations. On the other hand, see the same numbered chapter of *Liber Aleph*:

> *DE CORDE CANDIDO*
> *Think also, o my Son, of this Image, that if two States be at Peace, a Man goeth between them without Let; but if there be War, all Gateways are forthwith closed, save only for a few, and these are watched and guarded, so that the Obstacles are many. This then is the Case of Magick; for if thou have brought to Harmony all Principles within thee, thou mayst work easily to transmute a Force into its semblable upon another Plane, which is the essential Miracle of our Art; but if thou be at War within thyself, how canst thou work? For our Master Hermes Trismegistus hath written at the Head of His Tablet of Emerald this Word: That which is above is like that which is below, and that which is below is like that which is above, for the Performance of the Miracle of the One Substance. How then, if these be not alike? If the Substance of Thee be Two, and not One? And herein is the Need of the Confession of a pure Heart, as is written in the Book of the Dead.*

HLL is shone, gloried, praised:

> *ADNI. In Roman characters LXV = LVX, the redeeming light. See the 5° = 6° ritual and 'Konx om Pax'. Note 65 = 13 × 5, the most spiritual form of force, just as 10 × 5 was its most material form. Note HS, 'Keep silence!' and HIKL, the palace; as if it were said 'Silence is the House of Adonai'.*
>
> (*The Temple of Solomon the King*)

MKH is a beating or striking, MSVZH is a door post, the door being Atu III, Venus.

We leave the final word to the *Book of Lies*:

SIC TRANSEAT

At last I lifted up mine eyes, and beheld; and lo! the flames of violet were become as tendrils of smoke, as mist at sunset upon the marsh-lands. 'And in the midst of the moon-pool of silver was the Lily of white and gold. In this Lily is all honey, in this Lily that flowereth at the midnight. In this Lily is all perfume; in this Lily is all music. And it enfolded me'. Thus the disciples that watched found a dead body kneeling at the altar. Amen!

COMMENTARY

65 is the number of Adonai, the Holy Guardian Angel; see Liber 65, Konx Om Pax, and other works of reference.

The chapter title means, 'So may he pass away', the blank obviously referring to NEMO.

The 'moon-pool of silver' is the Path of Gimel, leading from Tiphareth to Kether; the 'flames of violet' are the Ajna Chakkra; the lily itself is Kether, the lotus of the Sahasrara. 'Lily' is spelt with a capital to connect with Laylah.

66

The number of verses in Chapter 1 of the *Book of the Law*, and 'The Mystic Number of the Qliphoth, and of the Great Work'. See the Comment to *Liber AL*, I.1, above.

ALHYK refers to 'The Lord thy God (is a consuming fire) Deut IV: 24' and see *The Ritual for the Evocation of Taphthartharath*.

ANYH a ship metaphor for thoughts that move in the unconscious.

DE CONFORMITATE MAGI

See to it therefore, o my Son, that thou in thy Working dost no Violence to the whole Will of the All, or to the Will common to all those Beings (or By-comings) that are of one general Nature with thee, or to thine own particular Will. For first of all thou art necessarily moved toward the One End from thine own Station, but secondly thou art moved toward the End proper to thine own Race, and Caste, and Family, as by Virtue of thy Birth. And these are, I may say it, Conditions or limits, of thine own individual Will. Thou dost laugh? Err not, my Son! The Magus, even as the Poet is the Expression of the true Will of his Fellows, and his Success is his Proof, as it is written in 'The Book of the Law'. For his Work is to free Men from the Fetters of a false or a superannuated Will, revealing unto them, in Measure attuned to their Needs, their true Natures.

(Liber Aleph)

BChVN is a trial or experiment, while GLGL is the wheel, surname of the Shekinah. KMV shows similitude, VS, us, while NBZBH is a gift or reward. See *Liber Stellæ Rubeæ sub figura LXVI*. Once again, the *Book of Lies* is useful.

THE PRAYING MANTIS

Say: 'God is One'. This I obeyed: for a thousand and one times a night for one thousand nights and one did I affirm the Unity. But 'night' only means LAYLAH; and Unity and GOD are not worth even her blemishes. Allah is only sixty-six; but LAYLAH counteth up to Seven and Seventy. 'Yea! the night shall cover all; the night shall cover all'.

COMMENTARY

66 is the number of Allah; the praying mantis is a blasphemous grasshopper which caricatures the pious.

The chapter recurs to the subject of Laylah, whom the author exalts above God, in continuation of the reasonings given in Chapter 56 and 63. She is identified with NOX by the quotation from Liber 65.

NOTES

(34) Laylah is the Arabic for night.

(35) A L L H = 1 + 30 + 30 + 5 = 66. L + A + I + L + A + H = 77, which also gives MZL, the Influence of the Highest, OZ, a Goat, and so on.

(Chapter 66, Book of Lies)

67

Binah, Understanding, the third sephirah, the Great Sea, it is also the number of ZYN, the Sword of division, Atu VI. 67 is a prime.

DE POETIS

For this Reason is the Poet called an Incarnation of the Zeitgeist, that is, of the Spirit or Will of his Period. So every Poet is also a Prophet, because when that which he sayeth is recognized as the Expression of their own Thought by Men, they translate this into Act, so that, in the Parlance of the Folk vulgar and ignorant, 'that which he foretold is come to pass'.

Now then the Poet is Interpreter of the Hieroglyphs of the Hidden Will of Man in many a matter, some light, some deep, as it may be given unto him to do. Moreover, it is not altogether in the Word of any Poem, but in the quintessential Flavour of the Poet, that thou mayst seek this Prophecy. And this is an Art most necessary toe every Statesman. Who but Shelley foretold the Fall of Christianity, and the Organisation of Labour, and the Freedom of Woman; who by Nietzsche declared the Principle at the Root of the World-War? See thou clearly then that in these Men were the Keys of the Dark Gates of the Future; Should not the Kings and their Ministers have taken heed thereto, fulfilling their Word without Conflict.

(Liber Aleph)

SODOM-APPLES

I have bought pleasant trifles, and thus soothed my lack of LAYLAH. Light is my wallet, and my heart is also light; and yet I know that the clouds will gather closer for the false clearing. The mirage will fade; then will the desert be thirstier than before. O ye who dwell in the Dark Night of the Soul, beware most of all of every herald of the Dawn! O ye who dwell in the City of the Pyramids beneath the Night of Pan, remember that ye shall see no more light but That of the great fire that shall consume your dust to ashes!

COMMENTARY

This chapter means that it is useless to try to abandon the Great Work. You may occupy yourself for a time with other things, but you will only increase your bitterness, rivet the chains still on your feet.

Paragraph 4 is a practical counsel to mystics not to break up their dryness by relaxing their austerities.

The last paragraph will only be understood by Masters of the Temple.

67 contains an alchemical formula:

YZN preparations: ZLL debased, TChN grind or reduce to a powder, KMZ make into a roundish form, ChNT to embalm.

(Chapter 67, Book of Lies)

68

S8 is the abbreviation used by members of the Society of Eight.

Nuit is Infinite Extension; Hadit Infinite Contraction. Khabs is the House of Hadit, even as Nuit is the house of Khu, and the Khabs is in the

Khu AL I.8. These theologies reflect mystic experiences of Infinite Con-traction and Expansion, while philosophically they are the two opposing Infinities whose interplay gives Finity.

(Old Comment to *AL*, II.2)

The symbol for infinity is 8 on its side. See the 2 of Disks.

DE MAGIS ORDINIS A.·. A.·. quibus caro fit verbum
Now, o my Son, the Incarnation of a Poet is particular and not Universal; he sayeth indeed true Things but not the Things of All-Truth. And that these may be said it is necessary that One take human Flesh, and become a Magus in our Holy Order. He then is called the Logos, or Logos Aiones, that is to say, the Word of the Aeon or Age, because he is verily that Word. And thus may be known, because He hath it given unto Him to prepare the Quintessence of the Will of God, that is, of Man, in its Fullness and Wholeness, comprehending all Planes, so that his Law is simple, and radi-cal, penetrating all Space from its single Light. For though His Words be many, yet is His Word One, One and Alone; and by this Word he createth Man anew, in an essential Form of Life, so that he is changed in his inmost Knowledge of himself. And this Change worketh outwards, little by little, unto its visible Effect.

(*Liber Aleph*)

See also the *Book of Lies*, Manna, Chapter 68.

It is remarkable that this extraordinary Experience has practically no effect upon the normal consciousness of The Beast. 'Intoxicate the inmost, o my God'—and it was His Magical Self, 666, that was by this Ecstasy initi-ated. It needed years for this Light to dissolve the husks of accident that shrouded his True Seed.

(The New Comment to *AL*, II.68)

68 is the number of being wise.

69

69 = ABVS, a manger, stable, enclosure. This Aethyr describes the Place of the Preliminary Ceremony of the Initiation of the Master of the Temple. The Candidate is fortified for the Ordeal of Intimate Communion with his

Holy Guardian Angel, who comes upon him unaware, and prepares him
interiorly below any normal sphere of consciousness.

(Note to ZEN, *Liber 418*)

70

The number of the first Aethyr *LIL*

In Hebrew letters the name of the Aethy is 70, Ayin; but by turning
the Yetziratic attributions of the letters into Hebrew, it gives 66, and
66 is the sum of the numbers from 0 to 11.)

(Note to *LIL*, *Liber 418*)

DE GAUTAMA
Whom Men call Gotama, or Siddartha, or the Budha, was a Magus of
our Holy Order. And His Word was Anatta; for the Root of His whole
Doctrine was that there is no Atman, or Soul, as Men ill translate it,
meaning a Substance incapable of Change. Thus, He, like Lao-Tze, based
all upon a Movement, instead of a fixed Point. And His Way of Truth was
Analysis, made possible by great Intention of the Mind toward itself, and
that well fortified by certain tempered Rigour of Life. And He most thor-
oughly explored and Mapped out the Fastnesses of the Mind, and gave the
Keys of its Fortresses into the Hand of Man. But of all this the Quintes-
sence is in this one Word Anatta, because this is not only the foundation
and the Result of his whole Doctrine, but the Way of its Work.

(*Liber Aleph*)

70 is Atu XV, an eye and ADNYH, Adonai with an H. It is a Secret, wine,
Night and silence:

Hadit is hidden in Nuit, and knows Her, She being an object of knowl-
edge; but He is not knowable, for He is merely that part of Her which She
formulates in order that She may be known.

(The New Comment to *AL*, II.4)

71

ADVNY Lord (i.e. Adonai) who is ALM silent. The vision ChZN of LAM.

DE SRI KRISHNA ET DE DIONYSO
Krishna has Names and Forms innumerable, and I know not His true Human Birth, for His Formula is of the Major Antiquity. But His Word hath spread into many Lands, and we know it today as INRI with the secret IAO concealed therein. And the Meaning of this Word is the Working of Nature in Her Changes; that is, it is the Formula of Magick whereby all Things reproduce and recreate themselves. Yet this Extension and Specialisation was rather the Word of Dionysus; for the true Word of Krishna was AUM, importing rather a Statement of the Truth of Nature than a practical Instruction in detailed Operations of Magick. But Dionysus, by the Word INRI, laid the Foundation of all Science, as We say Science to-day in a particular Sense, that is, of causing external Nature to change in Harmony with our Wills.

(Liber Aleph)

71 is the number of fullness MLA and a dove YVNH.

72 ADNY transliterated as by Lemegeton

It follows that, as Hadit can never be known, there is no death. The death of the individual is his awakening to the impersonal immortality of Hadit. This applies less to physical death than to the Crossing of the Abyss; for which see Liber 418, Fourteenth Aethyr.

(The New Comment to *AL* II.6)

72 is The NAME, which is also Chesed ChSD.

DE TAHUTI
Tahuti, or Thoth, confirmed the Word of Dionysus by continuing it; for he showed how by the Mind it was possible to direct the Operations of the Will. By Criticism and by recorded Memory Man avoideth Error. But the true Word of Tahuti was AMOUN, whereby He made Men to understand their secret Nature, that is, their Unity with their true Selves, or, as they then phrased it, with God. And He discovered unto them the Way of this Attainment, and its Relation with the Formula of INRI. Also by His Mystery of Number He made plain the Path for His Successor to declare the Nature of the whole Universe in its Form and in its Structure,

as it were an Analysis thereof, doing for Matter what the Buddha was decreed to do for Mind.

(*Liber Aleph*)

The number of the letters of Shemhamphorash, the 'Divided Name', i.e. Tetragrammaton in detail. Also, 72 = Beth Ayin, the 'Secret Nature' of Atziluth, the Archetypal World of Pure Reality.

(ZEN, *Liber 418*)

73

The Chokmah Days: 5 × 73 = 365. The number of Gimel, Atu II. A day of feast, and the power of Yetsirah. Also the River Gihon.

DE QUODAMM MAGO AEGYPTIORUM—QUEM APPELUNT JUDAEI MOSHEH

The Follower of Tahuti was an Egyptian whose Name is lost; but the Jews called Him Mosheh, or Moses, and their Fabulists made Him the Leader of their Legendary Exodus. Yet they preserved His Word, and it is YHVH, which thou must understand also as that Secret Word which thou hast seen and heard in Thunders and Lightnings in thine Initiation to the Degree thou wottest of. But this Word is itself a Plan of the Fabrick of the Universe, and upon it hath been elaborated the Holy Qabalah, whereby we have Knowledge of the Nature of all Things soever upon every Plane of By-coming, and of their Forces and Tendencies and Operations, with the Keys to their Portals. Nor did He leave any Part of His Work unfinished, unless it be that accomplished three hundred Years ago by Sir Edward Kelly, of whom I also come, as thou knowest.

(*Liber Aleph*)

KEFALH OG THE DEVIL, THE OSTRICH, AND THE ORPHAN CHILD

Death rides the Camel of Initiation Thou humped and stiff-necked one that groanest in Thine Asana, death will relieve thee! Bite not, Zelator dear, but bide! Ten days didst thou go with water in thy belly? Thou shalt go twenty more with a firebrand at thy rump! Ay! all thine aspiration is to death: death is the crown of all thine aspiration. Triple is the cord of silver moonlight; it shall hang thee, O Holy One, O Hanged Man, O Camel-Termination-of-the-third-person-plural for thy multiplicity, thou Ghost of a Non-Ego! Could but Thy mother behold thee, O thou UNT The Infinite Snake Ananta that surroundeth the Universe is but the Coffin-Worm!

COMMENTARY

Paragraph 4 identifies the reward of initiation with death; it is a cessation of all that we call life, in a way in which what we call death is not. 3, silver, and the moon, are all correspondences of Gimel, the letter of the Aspiration, since Gimel is the Path that leads from the Microcosm in Tiphareth to the Macrocosm in Kether.

(Chapter 73, *Book of Lies*)

74

74 is an Ox-Goat LMD, Atu VIII, a circuit SBYB and constantly OD.

All the way, constantly. The magical light. Od is the positive form of OB. Its number 11 identifies it with the light of Daath or death, and therefore with the formula of magick, or energy tending to change.

(*Liber 58*)

CAREY STREET

When NOTHING became conscious, it made a bad bargain. This consciousness acquired individuality: a worse bargain. The Hermit asked for love; worst bargain of all. And now he has let his girl go to America, to have 'success' in 'life': blank loss. Is there no end to this immortal ache That haunts me, haunts me sleeping or awake? If I had LAYLAH, how could I forget Time, Age, and Death? Insufferable fret! Were I an hermit, how could I support The pain of consciousness, the curse of thought? Even were I THAT, there still were one sore spot—The Abyss that stretches between THAT and NOT. Still, the first step is not so far away:—The Mauretania sails on Saturday!

COMMENTARY

Paragraphs 1–4 are in prose, the downward course, and the rest of the chapter in poetry, the upward. The first part shows the fall from Nought in four steps; the second part, the return.

    The details of this Hierarchy have already been indicated in various chapters. It is quite conventional mysticism.

    Step 1, the illumination of AIN as Ain Soph Aour; step 2, the concentration of Ain Soph Aour in Kether; step 3, duality and the rest of it down to Malkuth; step 4, the stooping of Malkuth to the Qliphoth, and the consequent ruin of the Tree of Life.

(Chapter 74, *Book of Lies*)

DYYN is a leader or judge: *Liber Testis Testitudinis* vel ‏ד י‎ sub figurâ LXXIV, while YSD creates a seat or foundation.

75

DE SE IPSO

O my son! me seemeth in certain Hours that I am myself fallen on a Time even more fearful and fatal than did Mahommed, peace be upon Him! But I read clearly the Word of the Aeon, that is ABRAHADABRA, wherein is the whole Mystery of the great Work, as thou knowest. And I have 'The Book of the Law', that was given unto me by Him thou wottest of; and it is the Interpretation of the Secret Will of Man on every Plane of his By-coming; and the Word of the Law is THELEMA. 'Do what thou wilt shall be the whole of the Law'. Now because 'Love is the law, love under will'. do I write this Epistle for thee, that thou mayst fulfil this inmost Will of Mankind, making them capable of Light, Live, Love and Liberty by the Acceptance of this Law. And the Hindrance thereunto is but as the Shell of its Egg to an Eaglet, ad Thing foreign to itself, a Protection till the Hour strike, and then—no more!

(*Liber Aleph*)

75 is Laylah the Night, Lucifer and the Pleiades, NUIT the Star Goddess and colours. 75 is Cohen, the priest.

PLOVERS' EGGS

Spring beans and strawberries are in: goodbye to the oyster!

If I really knew what I wanted, I could give up Laylah, or give up everything for Laylah. But 'what I want' varies from hour to hour.

(*Book of Lies*)

220

220 is the number of verses of The Book of the Law: And this book brings about the disruption described in this Aethyr.

(Comment to RII, *Liber 418*)

Ye shall cleave unto YHVH. The Elect. Giants.

418 (4 + 1 + 8 = 13)

418 = ATh IAV, the Essence of IAO, q.v.
(The Temple of Solomon the King, Chapter 5)

The gematria value of MAKAShANA ('The Word of the Aeon') and Cheth (a fence, the 8th letter) is 418.

The most vital Triad

Pages 284 to 287 are dedicated to Triads. The Triad is an obvious triangle, as are 1, 2, and 3; these numbers sum to 6 which takes us to Tipareth. Not a bad thing-in-itself, but Crowley had a better sequence, 0, 1, 2, the sum of which is 3, Binah, the City of the Pyramids. Obviously this keeps everything in the Supernal Triangle, which is just as well for a triangle with zero on one side is not a triangle.

Note how Crowley comments on all of these permutations except 102.

201

Part II The Universe as we seek to make it
201 AR, Light (Chaldee). Note 201 = 3 × 67, Binah, as if it were said, 'Light is concealed as a child in the womb of its mother'. The occult retort of the Chaldean Magi to the Hebrew sorcerers who affirmed AVR, Light, 207, is holy enough.
(Liber 58)

This is a perfect commentary of the numbers 0, 1, 2 above.

Consider the following permutations of these numbers in the Supernal Triangle and pertaining to Binah.

102

- AMVNH Truth, faith, trust
- AVVZ LBN A white goose
- BOL Lord, a King of Edom

- BQ Make empty or void
- NChMD Longed for
- OKBYS Spider
- TzBY Grace, fame, Goat
- YTzB Place firmly
- MAYAN a magician

210

210 = Sum 1 – 20

Section IV
210 Pertains to Part II. See *Liber 418*.

Part II The Universe as we seek to make it
210 Upon this holiest number it is not fitting to dilate. We may refer Zelatores to Liber VII. Cap. I., Liber Legis Cap. I., and Liber 418. But this was only revealed later. At first I only had ABRAHA, the Lord of the Adepts. Cf. Abraha-Melin.

(*Liber 58*)

OMPEHDA, see *AL*, III.54.

BChR Choice, to have pleasure, to love BRCh Pass on, fly ChBR Incantations, brother ChRB A sword DVR Cycle, generation HRH To conceive NOTz NOX QYQ Empty vessel, place void of matter RChB Space, place RY Spiritual emanation

0.12

Dividing 6/50 = 0.12. 0, the circumference, Nuit.., the centre, Hadit. 1, the Unity proceeding, Ra-Hoor-Khuit. 2, the Coptic H, whose shape closely resembles the Arabic figure 2, the breath of Life, inspired and expired. Human consciousness, Thoth. Adding 50 + 6 = 56, Nu, and Concentrating 5 + 6 = 11, ABRAHADABRA, etc. Multiplying 50 × 6 = Shin, and Ruach Elohim, the Holy Spirit.

(Commentary on *AL*, I.1, 'Nu! The Hiding of Hadit')

The greatest number is 120.

120

120 Sum equivalent to the 5th Path (Geburah).

Section IV

*120 SMK, Samech, a prop. Also MVSDI, basis, foundation. 120 = 1 ×
2 × 3 × 4 × 5, and is thus a synthesis of the power of the pentagram.
(Also 1 + 2 + ... + 15 = 120.) Hence its importance in the 5° = 6° ritual,
q.v.supra Equinox III. I however disagree in part; it seems to me to symbolise a lesser redemption than that associated with Tiphereth. Compare
at least the numbers 0.12 and 210 in Liber Legis and Liber 418, and extol
their superiority. For while the first is the sublime formula of the infinite
surging into finity, and the latter the supreme rolling-up of finity into
infinity, the 120 can symbolise at the best a sort of intermediate condition
of stability. For how can one proceed from the 2 to the 0? 120 is also ON,
a very important name of God.*

(*Liber 58*)

12

Section IV
*12 HVA, 'He', a title of Kether, identifying Kether with the Zodiac, and
'home of the 12 stars' and their correspondences. See 777.*

(*Liber 58*)

21

Section IV
*21 AHIH, existence, a title of Kether, Note 3 × 7 = 21. Also IHV, the first
3 (active) letters of IHVH. Mystic number of Tiphereth.*
    Part II The Universe as we seek to make it
    21 As bad, nearly, as 7.

(*Liber 58*)

CHAPTER FIFTEEN

The martial nature of Adonai

Yea, verily, I the Lord Viceregent of His Kingdom, I, Adonai, who speak unto my servant V.V.V.V.V. did rule and govern in His place.

(ARARITA, 1907)

Aleister Crowley makes the surprising point that Adonai is martial, when we might consider it to be Solar. How he comes to that conclusion is found in the Magic Square of Mars.

11	24	7	20	3
4	12	25	8	16
17	5	13	21	9
10	18	1	14	22
23	6	19	2	15

The central cross sums to 65, while arms of the cross sum to 26. Furthermore, the outer arms 17/9 and 7/19 both add to 26. The central square is 13, AChD or AHBH, which also sum to 65.

These numbers are discussed at length on page 4 of the *Book of Thoth*.

Another perfect form found in the square of Mars is the Svastika.

11	24	7	20	3
4	12	25	8	16
17	5	13	21	9
10	18	1	14	22
23	6	19	2	15

The arms of the Svastika form the basic moves of the Knight on a chess board.

Another way of looking at the arms is $4 \times L = 4 \times 30 = 120$ an important number.

Either way, the form of quadrants is reminiscent of the quarters around the North Pole and the Aces. However, Crowley describes this system in Atu VII which connects to *Liber 418*:

> The pillars are the four pillars of The Universe, the regimen of Tetragrammaton. The scarlet wheels represent the original energy of Geburah which causes the revolving motion. This chariot is drawn by four sphinxes composed of the four Kerubs, the Bull, the Lion, the Eagle and the Man. In each sphinx these elements are counter-changed; thus the whole represents the sixteen sub-elements.

These are the sums of the arms:

Fire: 11 + 24 + 7 + 25 = 67 Water: 3 + 16 + 9 + 21 = 49 Air: 5 + 17 + 10 + 23 = 55 Earth: 1 + 19 + 2 + 15 = 37

67 is the number of the Great Mother—Binah. Note 6 + 7 = 13 Unity as does 4 + 9 49 is the number of Venus 55 is the Mystic Number of Malkuth 37 is the highest principle of the soul attributed to Kether.

55 and 37 sum to 10.

The sum of the numbers is 208, with the addition of a zero is 2080 the number of Mercury.

The 8 empty squares are 16, 28, 24 and 36 which is 104, half 208, the number of Tzaddi.

A 3D form of the Svastika gives 70 squares, the number of the Eye and Atu XV. The addition of the 8 squares gives 78.

CHAPTER SIXTEEN

Crowley's Kantian worldview

The influence of Immanuel Kant on Crowley can be seen by the use of phrases such as *'ding an sich'* and the 'order of things' as part of his doctrine of categories, which appear in the *Book of Thoth*.

Kant is best known for his rigid views on ethics and morality, which makes Crowley's espousal of this philosopher surprising to those who think Crowley was a Satanist. In fact, Crowley had high moral standards as can be seen by his rejection of Mathers and in upholding the law.

Kant's views on religion seeps into the Crowleyian ethos, as seen by the maxims found in the *Book of the Law*, such as 'The law is for all', 'Do what thou wilt shall be the whole of the law', which are designed to be completely inclusive. Very Kantian.

Crowley shares a strong belief in the power of logic and the use of mathematics, hence the inclusion of algebraic formulae in the *Book of Thoth* and the importance of numbers. Geometry is another area shared with the Freemasons.

Kant's influence on the theory of art continue to this day. Kant considered poetry to be the highest of the arts which reflects Crowley's passion for this form.

The origin for Crowley's views on spirits (which he never states) is found in *Dreams of a Spirit-Seer* (1766) a little-known book by

Immanuel Kant, who was in turn influenced by Emanuel Swedenborg (1688–1772). Kant has no doubt in the existence of spirits; his concern is how they are perceived and the power of dreams.

> *In his theology he asserts the absolute unity of God in both essence (essentia) and being (esse). The Father, the Son, and the Holy Spirit represent a trinity of essential qualities in God; love, wisdom, and activity. This divine trinity is reproduced in human beings in the form of the trinity of soul, body, and mind.*
>
> (*Encyclopedia Brittanica* online)

Swedenborg's espousal of the Trinity is important in the higher forms of Freemasonry, and for example in pp. 285–287 of the *Book of Thoth*.

His influence on Freemasonry is seen in the mysterious Swedenborgian Rite, where experts agree that Swedenborg was never a Freemason.

However, the reason why Freemasons including Crowley would be fascinated by Swedenborg is obvious by reading *Earths In Our Solar System Which Are Called Planets, and Earths In The Starry Heaven Their Inhabitants, And The Spirits And Angels There* (1860).

The thing-in-itself

There is a common link between various aspects that appear to be isolated. Examples are the two 'Naples Arrangement', the 'Star Sponge Vision', *The Book of the Great Auk*, *Liber AL*, number theory, number formulae, geometry, the different viewpoint from A to B, the Tzaddi transposition, and so on.

All these disparate sections are linked to the theories of Immanuel Kant (1724–1804), in particular '*ding an sich*', the thing-in-itself or things-in-themselves. This is by no means a random set of ideas, or a fly-by-night whim. Crowley has been working with the notion since the first decade of the 20th century. Crowley mentions the 'thing-in-itself' several times in the *Book of Thoth* so we know it is important.

Crowley's practical application of *ding an sich* is key to his undisputed clairvoyant techniques and insights, including the visions of *Liber 418* and Abra-melin and many other documents. Put another way, in the absence of any valid theory of how the Tarot works, ding an sich is the methodology that Crowley establishes by the examples above.

CHAPTER SEVENTEEN

Shadow work

Mastering the Reason, he becomes as a little child, and invokes his Holy Guardian Angel, the Augoeides.

(*AHA!*, 1912)

The Shadow is a constant that never leaves us. The Shadow represents all that we have not assimilated into the Self. Magical and spiritual work exacerbates or manifests all that is represented in the Shadow; it is pernicious, frustrating, very difficult to deal with. Internally the Shadow manifests as negative feelings such as sadness, anger, laziness or cruelty. Externally the Shadow manifests as situations that never seem to get resolved, or a person from the family, or in the form of enemies. The group is another dynamic. Carl Jung coined the concept of the Shadow.

Magicians tend to see the Shadow in the forms of demons that they battle with, in evocations or invocations. Ultimately, acceptance and the ability to work with the Shadow is the corollary of finding one's Augoeides or Holy Guardian Angel, expressed alchemically as solve et coagula.

Unfortunately, in order to find one's Augoeides the Shadow has to be dealt with. Expression of the mere intention to find the Hidden Masters or Secret Chiefs will trigger the Shadow into action. Most people discover the Shadow through psychotherapy. (Most people who come to me for a tarot consultation are in the throes of dealing with the Shadow—Tarot is excellent for this.). Working with or on the Shadow is solitary—group work will only exacerbate or antagonise the Shadow.

Aleister Crowley had a very happy childhood until the death of his father after which he was shunted around various relatives. He escaped to Cambridge, but he soon tired of the companionship of his fellow undergraduates, preferring to dine alone rather than in the grand hall. The *Cloud Upon the Sanctuary* by Karl von Eckartshausen inspired Crowley on his journey to find the Hidden Masters. Crowley left Cambridge before completing his degree. Mountaineering was his passion, which is interesting in itself for climbing the mountain is a classic description of the path.

Oscar Eckenstein was Crowley's mountaineering guide literally and metaphorically.

The importance of Eckenstein is immortalised in *Liber Aleph*:

> *Thus I was brought unto the Knowledge of myself in a certain secret Grace, and as a Poet, by Jerome Politt of Kendal; Oscar Eckenstein of the Mountain discovered Manhood in me, teaching me to endure Hardship, and To Dare many Shapes of Death; also he nurtured me in Concentration, the Art of the Mystics, but without Lumber of Theology.*
>
> *(The Confessions of Aleister Crowley)*

Eckenstein sounds similar to Eckartshausen, at least to English ears; both were German, a nation that figures prominently in the story.

While snow-bound, Crowley read *The Kabbalah Unveiled* by MacGregor Mathers and didn't understand a word of it. Nevertheless, his interest was piqued. It was through another mountaineer, Julian L. Baker, an alchemist that the next stage of the journey began:

> *I had a number of conversations with Julian Baker, who kept his promise to introduce me to 'a man who was a much greater Magician than he was himself'. This was a Welshman, named George Cecil Jones. He possessed a fiery but unstable temper, was the son of a suicide, and bore a striking resemblance to many conventional representations of Jesus Christ. His spirit was both ardent and subtle. He was very widely read in Magick; and, being by profession an analytical chemist, was able to investigate the subject in a scientific spirit. As soon as I found that he really understood the*

matter I went down to Basingstoke, where he lived, and more or less sat in
his pocket. It was not long before I found out exactly where my destiny lay.
The majority of old magical rituals are either purposely unintelligible or
actually puerile nonsense. Those which are straightforward and workable
are, as a rule, better adapted to the ambitions of love-sick agricultural
labourers than those of educated people with a serious purpose. But there
is one startling exception to this rule. It is The Book of the Sacred Magick
of Abra-Melin the Mage.

(*The Confessions of Aleister Crowley*)

After admittance to the Hermetic Order of the Golden Dawn, Crowley
was once again reminded about Abra-melin:

IN THE AUTUMN of 1898 George Cecil Jones had directed the atten-
tion of Frater Perdurabo to a book entitled The Book of the Sacred Magic
of Abra-melin the Mage.

(*Book IV*, Part 4)

It was at one such Golden Dawn ceremony that Crowley espied and
recognised the power and magical talent of Allan Bennett standing
next to George Cecil Jones. Crowley rented a flat in Holborn for the
purposes of ritual and invocation of the Goetia using Mather's translation. Crowley insisted Bennett move into the flat after he discovered the
shocking poverty and squalor endured by the magician.

The three men worked on ritual magic, and in the meantime, Crowley
purchased Boleskine in Scotland as the pre-requisite for his practice of
the Abra-melin ritual—living in an isolated house.

By now Crowley had antagonised or scandalised the other members of the Golden Dawn with his bisexuality and attitude, except, of
course, for Mathers who had already adopted him as his protégé, surely
another bone of contention.

While at Boleskine Crowley received an urgent summons from
Mathers. Crowley returned on the overnight train to London in order
to retrieve magical regalia from the premises in Blythe Road, which
of course precipitated the expulsion of Mathers and Crowley in
January 1900.

For anyone else such an action would be devastating, but Crowley's
focus had already moved from the GD to Abra-melin and the ongoing
successful ritual work in Holborn.

Crowley had another string to his bow which mitigated the pain (if any) of separation from the GD. While 'rapidly advancing' through the GD degrees, invoking spirits in Holborn, and work on Abra-melin, Crowley was also working through the degrees of Freemasonry in Paris!

Sage advice would be to only pursue one of these ventures at a time— we can only admire Crowley's single-minded and dogged approach. Where the results came from is fairly easy to pinpoint. Crowley mentions his disappointment at 'learning the Hebrew alphabet' in the GD, while his memories of Freemasonry were of 'gobbledegook'.

Abra-melin was still in progress, which leaves us with the ritual work in Holborn as the primary driver of success in desire to converse with the Hidden Masters.

After the expulsion. Mathers directs Crowley to find new recruits in Mexico, a strange request unless, of course, Mathers wants him out of the way so he does not discover the truth, a classic case of the ends to the middle.

I had an introduction to an old man named Don Jesus Medina, a descendant of the great duke of Armada fame, and one of the highest chiefs of Scottish rite Freemasonry. My Cabbalistic knowledge being already profound by current standards, he thought me worthy of the highest initiation in his power to confer; special powers were obtained in view of my limited sojourn, and I was pushed rapidly through and admitted to the thirty-third and last degree before I left the country.

(The Confessions of Aleister Crowley)

I had also a certain amount of latitude granted by Mathers to initiate suitable people in partibus. I, therefore, established an entirely new Order of my own, called L.I.L.: the 'Lamp of the Invisible Light'. Don Jesus became its first High Priest. In the Order L.I.L., the letters L.P.D. are the monograms of the mysteries. An explanation of these letter is given by Dumas in the prologue of his Memoirs of a Physician, and Eliphas Levi discusses them at some length. I, however, remembered them directly from my incarnation as Cagliostro. It would be improper to communicate their significance to the profane, but I may say that the political interpretation given by Dumas is superficial, and the ethical suggestions of Levi puerile and perverse; or, more correctly, intentionally misleading. They conceal a number of magical formulae of minor importance by major practical value, and the curious should conduct such research as they feel impelled to make in the light of the Cabbala. Their numerical values, Yetziratic attributions,

and the arcana of the Atus of Tahuti, supply an adequate clue to such intel-
ligences as are enlightened by sympathy and sincerity.

(The Confessions of Aleister Crowley)

The general idea was to have an ever-burning lamp in a temple furnished
with talismans appropriate to the elemental, planetary and zodiacal forces
of nature. Daily invocations were to be performed with the object of mak-
ing the light itself a consecrated centre or focus of spiritual energy. This
light would then radiate and automatically enlighten such minds as were
ready to receive it.

(The Confessions of Aleister Crowley)

I devoted practically my whole time to this and other magical work.
I devised a Ritual of Self-Initiation, (The Book of the Spirit of the Living
God), the essential feature of which is the working up of spiritual enthusi-
asm by means of a magical dance.

(The Confessions of Aleister Crowley)

Furthermore, he visited some of the Enochian Aethyrs using large cards upon which were inscribed the squares of the Enochian Watchtowers.

While in Mexico he met up with his mentor Oscar Eckenstein for a spot of mountaineering. In the blink of an eye Crowley established his own Order and system of magic.

Back in Paris, Mathers showed Crowley the *Cipher Manuscript* as proof of the authenticity of Frau Sprengel in establishing the Hermetic Order of the Golden Dawn. However, Crowley had already been under astral attack (black magic) which he identified as coming from Mathers. Other attacks were from W.B. Yeats who was attacking Mathers too.

As if he needed further proof, the attacks combined with the success of the Temple of *LIL*, convinced Crowley to break all ties with the GD. Mathers was a formidable magician, and since Yeats was the new head of the GD, Crowley could never return.

Considering how badly he had been treated, it is surprising at the lack of rancour exhibited by Crowley. I think it is to do with the fact that he recognised the power and talent of Mathers to deceive all the members of the Golden Dawn including himself, which makes them victims, except of course they would not see it that way. Apart from George Cecil Jones and Allan Bennett, Crowley shunned contact with all the other members, except for A.E. Waite who was well known as an historian of Freemasonry and should know better.

CHAPTER EIGHTEEN

TARO as Tetragrammaton

Temple and Thora, Taro and Throa!
These are the goals and gates whereto ye tend,
O ribbed red barrows, whose virilia
Earn muliebria at the smooth sad end.
Alas! ye have not learned with God and me
To say your father's name A-dun-a-i!

(*Abjad-i-Al'ain*, 1910)

Aleister Crowley explores TARO, ROTA (the wheel), and TORA (the *Book of the Law*) in detail—they represent the perfect Triad. ATOR is Hathor goddess of love and of Venus.

Crowley says:

To show how these positions may be used in conjunction with the spirals, suppose that you are invoking Hathor, Goddess of Love, to descend upon the Altar. Standing on the square of Netzach you will make your invocation to Her, and then dance an inward spiral deosil ending at the foot of the altar, where you sink on your knees with your arms raised above the altar as if inviting Her embrace.

(*Book IV*, Part 3)

Hathor is the sacred cow, or pig. However, a name of far more signifi-cance is AHAThOOR, which is where things get a bit weird. To recap, the fourth position of the Tetragrammaton is the Daughter, final Heh or Earth position, who comes from a strange place, i.e. not from the three earlier positions.

AhaThOOR is 747, same as AVPNYM, wheels, and ZMN the appointed time, which together indicate a cyclical pattern, such as the Second Coming. Wheels correspond to TARO and ROTA, some would say a remarkable coincidence.

Ahathoor is also 361, ADNY H-ARTz, the initials are AHA, of which Crowley says:

> ADNI HARTz, the Lord of the Earth. Note 361 denotes the 3 Super-nals, the 6 members of Ruach, and Malkuth. This name of God therefore embraces all the 10 Sephiroth.

The final sentence refers to the astrological symbol of Venus which cov-ers all Sephiroth on the Tree of Life, mentioned in Atu III.

Breaking down AhaThOOR we again have AHA, a name of Venus, and AHA!

> The Sevenfold Mystery of the Ineffable Love; the Coming of the Lord in the Air as King and Judge of this corrupted World;
>
> (AHA!)

The exclamation mark causes the switch from Venus to Mercury, in other words 78.

Hoor 345 is Horus.

> MShH, Moses. Note that by transposition we have 543, AHIH AShR AHIEH, 'Existence is Existence', 'I am that I am', a sublime title of Kether. Moses is therefore regarded as the representative of this particular manifestation of deity, who declared himself under this special name.

Hoor therefore takes us from Malkuth to Kether, after another way. Also Hoor, who combines the force of the Sun with that of Mars. This is ADNY 65.

The missing letter is Teth, the serpent, Atu XI.

Control AhaThOOR and you control time, which Mathers and Crowley recognised.

In 1893 Mathers founded the Ahathoor temple in Paris. When Crowley was refused initiation into Adeptus Minor, Mathers took him to the temple to be initiated on 16 January 1900. Clearly Mathers had more control over the Ahathoor temple, which he continued to build upon.

Soon after, Mathers introduced Madame Horos as Frau Sprengel at the temple, which ultimately became the notorious Horos sex scandal. Horos is almost an anagram of Hoor.

Moving forward to April 1904 in Cairo with the reception of the *Book of the Law* where Rose Kelly was already pregnant with Crowley's first child Nuit Ma Ahathoor Hecate Sappho Jezebel Lilith, born on 28 July 1904, and who died barely two years old in Rangoon.

Apart from the dangers of naming a child with such potent names, Ahathoor is not a power to be messed with. Crowley no doubt recognised this when he wrote *AHA!* Ahathoor is the feminine goddess of Time, while Fortune, the better-known wheel of Fate.

747 is a deeply impersonal number. ZMN is also 97, an architect or building, Son of Man, Haniel, archangel of Netzach, quicksilver, and the names of several Goetic spirits. ChTP is to seize suddenly (the moment).

Perhaps this is why there is a table of 'The Meaning of the Primes from 11 to 97' in 777.

CHAPTER NINETEEN

The Formula of Tetragrammaton

The Formula of Tetragrammaton pops up many times in a number of disguises in the *Book of Thoth*.
Here is one from Atu 0:

> *It is necessary to acclimatise oneself to this at first sight strange, idea. As soon as one has made up one's mind to consider the feminine aspect of things, the masculine element should immediately appear in the same flash of thought to counterbalance it. This identification is complete in itself) philosophically speaking; it is only later that one must consider the question of the result of formulating Zero as 'plus 1 plus minus 1'. The result of so doing is to formulate the idea of Tetragrammaton.*

The Sephiroth are balanced through this formula.

> *The formula of Tetragrammaton is the most important for the practical magician. Here Yod = 2, He = 3, Vau = 4 to 9, He final = 10.*
>
> (*Book IV*, Part 3)

Kether (1) 'Kether is in Malkuth, and Malkuth is in Kether, but after another manner'. Chokmah (2) is Yod of Tetragrammaton, and therefore also Unity.

From which we derive 0=2.

Tiphereth (6) is the Hexagram, harmonizing, and mediating between Kether and Malkuth. Also it reflects Kether. 'That which is above, is like that which is below, and that which is below, is like that which is above'.

Malkuth (10) contains all the numbers, which includes the whole of Matter as we know it by the senses.

(*Book IV*, Part 3)

In terms of elements:

Yod, He, Vau, He, the Ineffable Name (Jehovah) of the Hebrews. The four letters refer respectively to the four 'elements', Fire, Water, Air, Earth, in the order named.

(*Book IV*, Part 3)

The formation of the 'Yod' is the formulation of the first creative force, of that father who is called 'self-begotten', and unto whom it is said: 'Thou has formulated thy Father, and made fertile thy Mother'. The adding of the 'He' to the 'Yod' is the marriage of that Father to the great co-equal Mother, who is a reflection of Nuit as He is of Hadit. Their union brings forth the son 'Vau' who is the heir. Finally the daughter 'He' is produced. She is both the twin sister and the daughter of 'Vau'.

His mission is to redeem her by making her his bride; the result of this is to set her upon the throne of her mother, and it is only she whose youthful embrace can reawaken the Eld of the All-Father. In this complex family relationship is symbolised the whole course of the Universe. It will be seen that (after all) the Climax is at the end. It is the second half of the formula which symbolises the Great Work which we are pledged to accomplish. The first step of this is the attainment of the Knowledge and Conversation of the Holy Guardian Angel, which constitutes the Adept of the Inner Order. The re-entry of these twin spouses into the womb of the mother is that initiation described in Liber 418, which gives admission to the Inmost Order of the A∴ A∴ Of the last step we cannot speak.

Crowley is referring to Binah, the City of the Pyramids.

In the 4 of Cups Crowley says:

> *Note also the refolding-in-upon-itself suggested by the 'Magic Number'*
> *of Four 1 + 2 + 3 + 4 which is Ten. Four is the number of the Curse of*
> *Limitation, of Restriction. It is the blind and barren Cross of equal arms,*
> *Tetragrammaton in his fatal aspect of finality, as the Qabalists knew him*
> *before the discovery of the Revolving Formula whereby the Daughter,*
> *seated upon the Throne of the Mother, 'awakens the Eld of the All-Father'.*

YHVH is completed in ALHYM:

> *'ALHYM', therefore, represents rather the formula of Consecration than*
> *that of a complete ceremony. It is the breath of benediction, yet so potent*
> *that it can give life to clay and light to darkness.*
>
> *In consecrating a weapon, 'Aleph' is the whirling force of the thunder-*
> *bolt, the lightning which flameth out of the East even into the West. This*
> *is the gift of the wielding of the thunderbolt of Zeus or Indra, the god of*
> *Air. 'Lamed' is the Ox-goad, the driving force; and it is also the Balance,*
> *representing the truth and love of the Magician. It is the loving care which*
> *he bestows upon perfecting his instruments, and the equilibration of that*
> *fierce force which initiates the ceremony.*
>
> *(Book IV, Part 3)*

One form of YHVH is Jeheshuah, Jesus the Redeemer, YHShVH.
Another is Amen, AMN 91:

> *91 = 7 × 13, the most spiritual form of the Septenary. AMN, Amen, the*
> *holiest title of God; the Amoun of the Egyptians. It equals IHVH ADNI*
> *(IAHDVNHI, interlaced), the eight-lettered name, thus linking the 7 to*
> *the 8. Note that AMN (reckoning N as final, 700) = 741 = AMThSh,*
> *the letters of the elements; and is thus a form of Tetragrammaton, a form*
> *unveiled.*

91 is the Mystic Number of Kether as Achad. See *Book of Lies*.
TARO is another form of the Tetragrammaton, expressed as ROTA
the wheel. While YHVH loops from Daughter to Mother, it is not complete in itself. To resolve this, Crowley added a paragraph to the *Book
of Thoth*:

The Pagan system is circular, self-generated, self-nourished, self-renewed. It is a wheel on whose rim are Father-Mother-Son-Daughter; they move about the motionless axis of Zero; they unite at will; they transform one into another; there is neither Beginning nor End to the Orbit; none is higher or lower than another. The Equation 'Naught=Many =Two= One= All= Naught' is implicit in every mode of the being of the System.

'Pagan' appears nowhere else in Crowley's writings, which suggests it is his idea of the circularity of YHVH and not from another source. The equation is an expansion of 0=2 as a complete expression of the Universe.

CHAPTER TWENTY

The initiated view of the *Book of Thoth*

U nderstanding the *Book of Thoth* is virtually impossible without the initiated viewpoint which starts with the Masonic Temple. Within the temple are two Pillars Yachin and Boaz which both have the value of 79. The base of Pillars is at Netzach and Hod, Venus and Mercury which have equal status. Multiplying Venus and Mercury, 7 × 8 = 56, or Nu (see *Liber AL*). Add the number of the letters of the Hebrew alphabet to 56 and we have 78, an important number in *Liber AL*.

Venus represents many septenaries, including the 'Days of the Week', seven planets and their corresponding magic squares. Mercury 8 represents the Mercurial gods including Thoth, Hermes, and Jesus Christ. 8 is equal to 7 (they are on the same level on the Kabalistic Tree of Life), but being one more, (718) corresponds to the Stele of Revealing. Crowley describes this as a black egg between the Pillars.

The *Book of Thoth* is designed around 7 and 8. All 78 cards and a tarot spread are represented by 7; these concepts are familiar to any tarot student. But the 8 is less well understood. Basically anything unfamiliar to the tarot student in the *Book of Thoth* falls under the aegis of 8.

Such a powerful and fundamental number as 78 naturally requires its own spirit. Aleister Crowley invoked Aiwas or AYVAS, who dictated the *Book of the Law* in the Great Pyramid.

The masculine and feminine character of the two Pillars is reflected in the Sephiroth at their base. Netzach is Fire, while Hod is Water, the two purifying elements used at the start of Golden Dawn rituals. In other words, the Tarot is invoked at beginning of the ritual.

M is water, while Sh is fire; forming ShM, the NAME which becomes the Divided Name or Shemhamphorash of 72 angels each ruling 5 degrees of the circle. Shin is 300, composed of ShYN, 360, the number of the circle, which gives us an equation. 360 = 0, or The Fool, which means that Judgment or The Aeon and The Fool are equivalent. This secret is hinted at with the transposition of Strength and Adjustment; Crowley continued this tradition in *Liber AL* with the statement 'Tzaddi is not the Star'. 4 × 90 = 360, while 4 × 91 (Amen or Amoun) takes us closer to the year. Zero is feminine in shape, the vesica piscis which is equivalent to the egg between the Pillars. The Fool is obviously masculine, but with the attribution of zero he is naturally bisexual giving rise to Crowley's favourite 0 = 2. The Fool is attributed to Aleph, which completes the Mother Letters, AMSh. Shin has the dual attribution of Spirit and Fire, ASh, which in English conveniently refers to the remains of Fire, the basis for the Mass of the Phoenix, (*Book of Lies*, Chapter 44), another number of 8 and to the Aethyr of MAZ where Crowley saw the Urn containing ash.

Returning to 360, divided by ten gives us the Minor Arcana on the Tree of Life. Five is required to complete the circle of the year.

Incidentally, Crowley included the designs from Eliphaz Levi of The Chariot and The Devil in his deck. The corresponding letters are Cheth and Ayin, or 8 and 70.

Circular patterns predominate. A good example is the word Tarot; according to Eliphas Levi the two T's indicate circularity—the final T takes us back to the beginning, which makes it redundant. TARO is the correct spelling, 671, the number of Adonai spelt in full.

Adonai is found in AGLA, which is also circular in nature.

The circle quartered is 90, which makes a cross or X within a circle, a symbol of Malkuth and part of the sigil of the A∴A∴. Tau 400 also means a cross and it is associated with Earth. Another version of the cross is the Ankh or Crux Ansata associated with the Hanged Man (water).

The dynamic form of the circle is the wheel (ROTA), while the spinning cross is represented by the Svastika formed of 17 squares (The Star). To commemorate this Crowley included Chapter 78 from the *Book of Lies* in the frontispiece.

The temple is rectangular in shape, while the Taro is circular. The Hebrew word for Temple is Beth, a house, which is also the letter B, Atu I The Magus. Together I0 represents the masculine and feminine, the Magus and The Fool. Ten is the number of Malkuth which completes the Tree of Life. Furthermore Atu X is The Wheel, while the 10th letter is Yod (Mercury rules Virgo), Atu IX. Beth is 2, secret attribution of the 2nd Sephirah Chokmah. Chokmah is usually considered to be the Zodiac, another circle. In other words Mercury rules both Hod and Chokmah, which sum to 10. Mercury is simultaneously above and below the Abyss on the Qabalistic Tree of Life. Astrologically, Mercury takes on the characteristics of the sign, planetary ruler, and other planets aspecting it.

Mercury is thus the perfect planet for invocations and rituals which are missing from Taro until Crowley included it in the *Book of Thoth*.

Returning to Cheth, the 8th letter, value is 418, the name of the *Liber* recording Crowley's travels through the 30 Aethyrs, extracts of some of them appear in the Appendix as well as in other places.

CHAPTER TWENTY ONE

Where is the TARO?

strange question! Crowley precisely locates the place of the
TARO in the tomb of Christian Rosenkreuz:

*The L Sign is the Svastika. (See Z in 0° = 0° Ritual for meaning.) Also
Svastika hath 17 squares showing IAO synthetical. And the Svastika
includeth the Cross, 'even as a child in the Womb of its Mother to develop
itself anew', (TOR). The Cubical Svastika hath 78 faces = 'Tarot' and
Mezla. It is also Aleph = 'Air' and Zero. It shows the Initiation of a
Whirling Force.*

*The V sign is that of Apophis and Typhon. It is the Y of Pythago-
ras; it is the arms flung up of the drowning man and therefore = '12th'
key and Mem. It is also the Horns of the mediaeval Devil. It shows the
binding and apparent death of the force, without which it cannot come to
any perfection.*

*The X sign is that of the Pentagram. It showeth the Triumph of the
Light. It is Shin descended, and therefore Fire. Moreover the Pentagram
formulateth the 10 Sephiroth. (Is not the Flaming Sword the Pentagram
unwound?) It is the final rise in perfect equilibrium of the force.*

*The whole is LVX. Showing the Light imperfect, until it hath descended
into Hell. (Sowing ___ waiting ___ reaping. Cyst reproduction of some*

simple animals. Hibernation, &c.) The arms are stretched out and then refolded ___ effort and peace. The Cross Sign shows Taw: and all four are thus AMThSh and AMN. The Vibrations pass with the Sun, of course. The Light being thus fixed in the Vault, all leave the same and the seal is given.

(*The Equinox*, III, *The Temple of Solomon the King*)

The sequence of paragraphs gives the elements Air, Water, Fire, and Earth, 741, which is Amoun or Amen, while the swastika is composed of four L's. $4 \times 30 = 120$. 120 is the sum of Chesed, Geburah and Tipareth, HUA $\times$ 10, and $1 \times 2 \times 3 \times 4 \times 5$, united in Earth.

Alternatively, we have:

- The Fool
- The Hanged Man
- The Aeon
- The Universe

'Pass with the Sun' is 360 degrees, or 365 days of the year.

CHAPTER TWENTY TWO

The End[1]

This chapter is a sort of final Confession of Faith. It is the unification of all symbols and all planes. The End is inexpressible.

(*Book of Lies*, Starlight)

The *Book of Thoth* is frustratingly opaque to Tarot students who base their authority in Mathers' Golden Dawn, including the Rider-Waite deck by A.E. Waite. However, when studied from Crowley's perspective, the *Book of Thoth* illuminates Mathers' system, the Rider-Waite tarot, and dare I say it, Thelema. In fact, the *Book of Thoth* is the Gateway to understanding Crowley's extensive writings.

Mathers deliberately kept the tarot in the Golden Dawn for divination purposes—nothing has changed to this day. Crowley was dead against using the *Book of Thoth* for divination purposes. The purpose of this deck is invocation, but Frieda Harris talked him out of including more on this important subject. Fortunately, their correspondence reveals the true purpose. Invocation using the *Book of Thoth* totally disempowers fraternities who sell membership on the basis of group ritual for initiation the ultimate revelation of 'secrets'. Fraternities have

---

[1] THE END = 78.

no control over solitary magicians who invoke. Crowley's keyword for initiation is Death, 'die daily'. Twice daily invocation of Mercury, Thoth, or Tahuti (they are all the same Spirit) results in personal initiation. Crowley even includes an invocation for Aiwass, Spirit of the Tarot.

Here is the equation: Invoke Mercury twice daily, experience initiation (die daily), and empower your life.

It was not a matter of 'if' but 'when' Crowley would write a book on the Tarot. 671 guaranteed that. Adonai has martial characteristics, which gives an interesting perspective on the nature of the Tarot.

Once Frieda Harris finally appeared, it was time to dust off the manuscript from the Cefalù days and update. Apart from the chaotic, almost comical events as related by the correspondence between Frieda Harris and Crowley, we learn little. Except of course that against her will Frieda Harris was required to invoke Mercury every day, a policy designed to cause chaos even if unintentionally. Despite not being a natural magician, it is clear that she channelled Tahuti to paint the cards. Mercury is the trickster after all.

671 is the enduring link from the Society of Eight to the present. Tahuti is Mercurial, while the martial energy of Adonai makes the system dynamic and magical. Invocation is a necessity.

What of Thelema? It is a word that appears only once in *Liber AL* in contrast to the *Book of Thoth* where it is depicted on the Ace of Swords and Atu VI. We might expect Thelema to make an appearance on the 2 of Wands, or at least the Ace of Wands, perhaps even Atu XVII. The Swords represent of division and conflict, another reason for Thelemites to take umbrage at this deck. Frieda Harris saw members of the O.T.O. as 'ecstatic idiots', and she determined to make sure the deck would stay in England, fortunately for us.

Aleister Crowley fought hard to liberate himself from the malign influence of MacGregor Mathers, which is why this book cannot be interpreted in terms of Mathers' system. Crowley documents the struggle for independence from Mathers culminating in the *Book of the Law* and beyond.

The reconstitution of Mather's Order demonstrates the victims were willing and compliant to his system, while Crowley was never popular with them, to say the least. It is not surprising that none of these members figure in Crowley's life—this is one of the unintended

conclusions of Tobias Churton's excellent books extensively document-
ing the personalities, none of whom were GD members.

Aleister Crowley eventually saw through Mathers' allegations and
reached out to Wynn Westcott, but Crowley's reputation made him
persona non grata. Here is the dilemma. Crowley's public personification
as 'the Beast' flies against acceptance within Freemasonry. As we know,
Crowley had a fruitful relationship with another Freemason, John
Yarker, but Yarker was not recognised by the United Grand Lodge of
England. The UGLE never recognised Crowley as a Freemason, despite
extensive correspondence which unfortunately has been lost.

The *Book of Thoth* brings together Kant's philosophy and speculative
Masonry which balances Thelema. The categorical imperative is the
foundation for moral law that applies to everyone: Crowley loves a
challenge, for he came up with his own moral maxims in the *Book of
the Law*.

CHAPTER TWENTY THREE

BABALON and ABRAHADABRA

Expressions of unity

Unity is AChD, 13, a number that is expressed in several important ways. The High Priestess, Gimel, is the 13th Path. The Hanged Man is Mem, the 13th letter of the Hebrew alphabet, while Nun is the letter associated with the 13th Atu.

3 × 13 is 39 of which Crowley says:

> *IHVH AChD, Jehovah is one. 39 = 13 × 3. This is then the affirmation of*
> *the aspiring soul.*

Twice 39 is 78; it would appear that 6 is the optimum number of stacks for a tarot spread, with 13 cards in each stack. The Unicursal Hexagram would be the optimum template for such a spread.

The sum of GMN is 93, a powerful Thelemic number.

The Priestess of the Silver Star connects Tipareth to Kether easily crossing the Abyss. The Hanged Man also represents transition to Adepthood. Death is strongly equated with initiation. These are the Keys to spiritual transformation.

Duality is of course the antithesis of Unity expressed as 11 which has greater potential for spreads. In theory there are ten permutations of spreads which correspond to the grade system the GD inherited from Freemasonry. The duality of 13 is 26, YHVH, the four elements, and the sum of the first four numbers as 10.

The form of each spread corresponds to the GD essay on polygons.

First Order

First Grade Neophyte 0° = 0°

In practice this grade refers to Malkuth, and the four elements, which arrive from another place (the Princesses), based upon YHVH, which is the First Operation of the Opening of the Key spread.

Zelator 1° = 10°

Ten stacks placed in circle below a solitary stack. Kether and Malkuth.

Theoricus 2° = 9°

Two stacks form a line, which can be oriented horizontally, vertically or at the angle from Chokmah to Kether. Below is a circle of nine stacks.

Practicus 3° = 8°

A triangle point down to represent Water over a circle of eight stacks.

Philosophus 4° = 7°

A square over a circle of seven stacks.

Second Order

Adeptus Minor 5° = 6°

Pentagram over a Hexagram.

Adeptus Major 6° = 5°

Hexagram over a Pentagram.

Adeptus Exemptus 7° = 4°

Heptagon over a square.

Third Order

Magister Templi 8° = 3°

Octagon over a triangle, point up.

Magus 9° = 2°

Nonagon over a line.

Ipsissimus 10° = 1°

Decagon over a point.

The Adeptus Minor spread is most useful; we know this because Crowley gives an example. The theme of the spread is death, transformation and reincarnation, free will versus fate. In this example the Hexagram pattern forms a reversed pentagram just to add an extra level of complexity. The power of six will resolve any negativity.

Adeptus Minor 5° = 6°

Spiritual Masters suffer violent deaths—Jesus Christ, Jacques de Molay, Hiram Abiff, John the Baptist—come to mind. Religious beliefs are often defined by such acts. There is a taboo amongst modern tarot readers to discuss death with clients, as if death is not part of life.

The purpose of the *Book of Thoth* as we know is not about fortune-telling or divination, but for invocation. Crowley even considered stipulating that the deck could only be sold with the book, but of course he died long before the deck was ever published.

In *A Devil of a Tale*, part of a series of stories published in *The Deuce and All* (1910) by George Raffalovich, we explore themes of violent death, ritual magic, Hindu black magic, the Golden Dawn, and predictions of suicide wrapped around a tarot reading!

The primary theme is reincarnation—Crowley believed he immediately reincarnated as Eliphas Levi, and perhaps he believed he too would suffer a violent death. As we know this prediction did not come true. Atu XV in the *Book of Thoth* is directly inspired by Levi's version.

At the start of the story, Crowley mentions Atus XII, XIII, and XVI, the combination of which immediately suggests termination. The Hanged Man represents the death of a Master and spiritual transformation, Death is a codeword for initiation, while The Tower depicts the destruction of a belief system among other things.

Exactly who the characters of the story represent in real life is ambiguous, unlike those in Moonchild which has been subject to greater study. Malcolm Graves is clearly Crowley, and note the sepulchral name. The Vault figures in the symbolism of Christian Rosenkreuz, the empty tomb in the Great Pyramid, so perhaps the entire story is an account of Adeptus Minor, 5° = 6°, which is not as fanciful as it sounds. Crowley attained this grade in 1904 at the same time as the reception of the *Book of the Law*.

The actual tarot reading suggests such an interpretation. The first part of the reading has only Major Arcana in five positions which reminds us of the Enochian Watchtowers of the Tablet of Union at the centre.

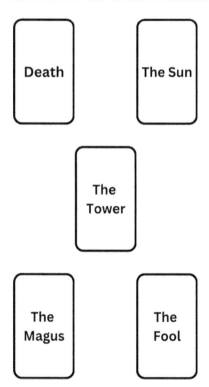

Crowley describes the tarot reading:

> Quickly caught as he was by the power of mystery, which had, from the beginning, impelled him towards magical practices, Malcolm Graves cut the cards with his left hand, then waited. He had at that moment the most absolute faith in whatever oracle was to be given him. He watched, and when the first selection by elimination had brought together on the table five hidden cards his heart started beating wildly, his eyes, swollen, were fixed on the point where his fortune—his fate—would be written as soon as the five hieroglyphics should be shown the light ...
>
> One by one, the cards were turned out by the adept, who glanced at them in silence, while breathing slowly and alternatively through his nostrils.
>
> Graves knew the individual meaning of these five hieroglyphics, but their association, their encounter, conveyed, as he had acknowledged, a much more complex meaning. He was about to put forth his version, when, suddenly and violently, the adept spread his hands over the cards.
>
> 'There is no need for your hiding them', Malcolm exclaimed, 'they tell only what any one may know. I am going to die soon'.
>
> (While turning the cards over, Graves was practising pranayama.)
>
> His tone was faintly sad. Death he welcomed—but life had still charms for him. The other man had removed his hands and turned his eye towards a second pack of five cards. Malcolm's words had had no effect on him; he inspected them, looked at them with eyes that perceived every particular; and at length he spoke.
>
> 'Mr. Graves, I am sorry not to have either the right or the power to hide these arcana from you. You have seen the first answer, and seem to understand it: your death will be the violent end of suicides, followed, as is the rule in similar cases, by an almost immediate reincarnation. I have seen the second pack, and as to the third one—there is no need for me to consult it. The cards may be hidden, yet I know them. They refer to myself. But enough! I prefer not to let you into this secret, which you will, alas, understand soon enough, I know how utterly useless would be my advice, and that my words are spoken too late. We shall meet again, and by that time I hope to master Fate and the spirits invisible. I must now leave you'.
>
> 'But, one moment, please', exclaimed the young man. 'You are most interesting! Do you think that I am a man to be frightened right away with a story of future meeting and reincarnation?'

(Iris Corbett is the lover of Malcolm Graves; She is 18 years old, the number of The Chariot in the Key Scale. A similar name, Osiris is the god of death,)

Was she boldly and foolishly carrying about a sign of evil, a symbol of Typhon, unaware of its meaning, or was she initiated—by god or man, it was all one and the same result—and did she know that Osiris is a dark god and Typhon his twin brother?

In *Liber 335*, Psyche describes Iris as:

I am a dewdrop focussing the sun That fires the forest to the horizon. I am a cloud on whom the sun begets The iris arch, a fountain in whose jets Throbs inner fire of the earth's heart, a flower Slain by the sweetness of the summer shower.

Analysing Osiris as OS and IRIS we have 130 and 280. 130 is the number of redemption, deliverance, and OYN, Eye 'The Secret of Generation is Death' another reference to The Devil.

280 is particularly significant. Of this number Crowley says:

7 × 40, the Squares on the walls of the Vault. See The Equinox, 3, p 222
Section IV
The sum of the 'five letters of severity', those which have a final form— Kaph, Men, Nun, Pe, Tzaddi. Also the number of the squares on the sides of the Vault 7 × 40; see 5° = 6° ritual. Also RP = terror.
Part II The Universe as we seek to make it
A grand number, the dyad passing to zero by virtue of the 8, the Charioteer who bears the Cup of Babalon. See Liber 418, 12th Aethyr. See also 280 in Part I.

The 'five letters of severity' refers to the five Makaras or panchama-kara: Mansa, Matsya, Madya, Maithuna, Mudra mentioned at the start of the tale. These are taboo substances used by Tantras of the Left-Hand Path.

Crowley's analysis of 280 clearly demonstrates that we are deal-ing with the Adeptus Major ritual associated with Mars and Geburah. Here is the point where the adepts has to make a choice between the Left-Hand Path and the Right-Hand Path. Sacrifice is required to progress.

The sum of these numbers, and therefore Osiris is 410, which has connotations of Visions, the Tabernacle, Holy, Sacred, and a Saint. The sum of 410 is five, the number of Mars and Geburah.

Metzareph is also 410, usually in conjunction with Aesch Mezareph, or Purifying Fire, an alchemical term derived from the Bible.

- ASh is fire, 301 a candlestick. ShA is a movement away from peace.
- The sum of 711 has no gematria.
- After that digression, let us return to the second tarot reading.

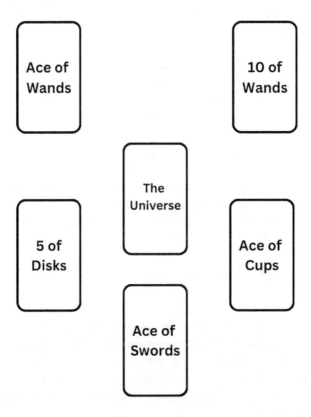

The cards are placed on an inverted pentagram, symbol of The Devil, with The World at the centre. The Universe is the matter at hand. The 5 of Coins is Martial, but note Mercury rules this card, while the 10 of Wands is oppression. The Three Aces indicate change, re-organisation.

The evening was close and stormy. He went out into the garden, and she sat at her little table by the window, watching him. Mechanically she took her pack of Tarot cards and placed six cards in the silver star. She looked at them for a minute and rose suddenly. She thought of the two men she knew. One—her lover—of whom she had yet said nothing; the other—her adopted father—who said he loved her … and who knew so much that she was almost afraid of him.

'Six cards in the silver star'. The first reading had five cards, the combination gives us 5° = 6°. Crowley attained Adeptus Minor in 1900 through MacGregor Mathers, while Adeptus was achieved in 1904 as previously stated. The Tale can therefore be seen as the transition from Mather's system to his own represented by the tradition of Eliphas Levi.

Priestess of the Silver Star is the magical title of the High Priestess; Iris is now acting in that exalted capacity, 'and rose suddenly'. The High Priestess is on the Path from the Sun, Tipareth to Kether, traversing the Abyss, another symbol of death to the ego.

Presently the storm broke. White and blue, red and yellow, gigantic, the forked lightning flashed over the hills. She called his name, but the Magician did not or would not hear. He marched out of the garden and ascended towards the storm. She wanted to run after him, but suddenly she felt that some event was taking place which she could not alter, which she was not to attempt to fight, and she stood silent, pale and sad.

'The storm broke … forked lightning', references to Atu XVI. 'She stood silent' she was in Kether. Note the alliteration.

He was going up, up towards the sky. She could see him at intervals. The lightning seemed to play around and above him, like vultures over a battlefield. Suddenly she saw him stop, lift his head. Daringly and gently, swiftly and softly, the point of flame touched him, messenger of Death, bringing the Kiss of Peace, the Light in Extension, to his saddened soul.

Symbols of death.

Yet he had not moved. She called for help, and they went after him. He was standing straight, his face to the sky, his eyes closed. She touched him

lightly on the shoulder, and the human frame that had been fell on the
soil—a handful of ashes.

Ashes, see *Book of Lies*, Chapter 44, The Urn, and the sixth Aethyr MAZ. The Urn suggests the identity of Iris to be one of Crowley's Scarlet Women.

The final act is located in the garden which brings to mind Adam and Eve. GN 53 comprises Death and the High Priestess while it is also 'The Number of Abra-Melin Servitors of Astarot and Asmodee' and 'The yoni as an instrument of pleasure'. ABN is the stone that slew Goliath, and ChMH the Sun. Also MAHBH a lover, NBA prophecy—see *Book of Lies*, Chapter 53.

Vision of 231 spread

Folios 54 and 55 of the *Cipher Manuscript* state the transposition of Justice and Strength without any reason or justification. Mathers who was entirely ignorant of the Tarot believed the justification was from a ritual point of view, and that is how it stayed ever since.

Aleister Crowley eventually transposed The Star with The Emperor, but I have often suspected without proof that he was emphasising the Society of Eight transposition. There is a short chapter, 'The Roman Numbers of the Trumps', where the footnote states that some of the paragraphs are deliberately repeated.

Bart Deleplanque's Vision of 231 casts an entirely different view. To go back to the Sepher Yetzirah, 231 is the number of pairs of the Hebrew letters, usually portrayed on a circle. But what would the pairing of the Atu look like? The natural method would be from 1 to 22, but of course The Fool is 0.

The Fool has to be zero for this new system to work, which is probably why the Roman numerals are the first column of page 278. The largest value for a pair in the Atu 231 is 41, XX + XXI, but since they are adjacent they are not paired. At the other end of scale 0 is paired with IX which sums to 9, the smallest value.

Hidden within this system is the reason why the Adepts of the Society of Eight transposed Strength and Justice, for if they were in their alphabetical positions in the new system breaks the symmetry. That Crowley preferred the use of Roman Numbers and their prominence in the table on page 278, worth breaking the order of Key Scale.

Liber 231 was published in 1907, an early document, and the basis for subsequent writings. There are four sections to *Liber 231*, reflecting Atu 231. Crowley might have figured out the Atu 231 himself, or he had access to other papers by the Society of Eight. This diagram may be key to how Crowley encoded future documents. Crowley emphasises mathematical proof as the basis of the Tarot, without offering such a proof.

The system hinges on the axis of X and XXI—elongating this axis flattens the diagram so it resembles The Double Loop in the Zodiac on page 11. Alternatively it resembles the *vesica piscis*.

However, this system is not just about pairing, for the sides also get summed, which is perhaps the best way to start.

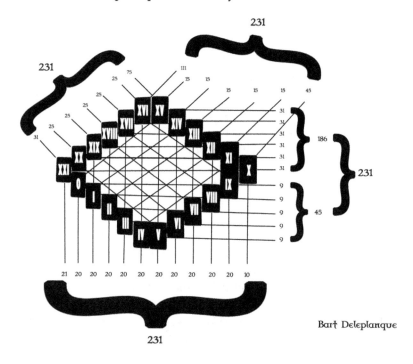

Bart Deleplanque

231 – 31

XXI, 0, I, II, III, IV = 31. This number requires no comment. The opposing side also sums to 31 in a different way, which gives us seven in total.

- XVI – XV
- XVII – XIV
- XVIII – XIII

- XIX – XII
- XX – XI
- XXI – X

The sum of these pairs is 186, the letter Qoph, PVQ to bring forth, MVSP an increase.

The other half to this sequence pairs to 9.

- 0 – IX
- I – VIII
- II – VII
- III – VI
- IV – V

The sum of these pairs is 45, the Mystic Number of Yesod, Adam, and Yetzirah.

186 + 45 = 231, which can be seen as Above and Below.

231 North-West

The North-West 231 is three sides of the square composed of 75 from the North-East side, 31 from the South-West side, and five pairs of 25.

We have already come across 31, moving onto 75 there is Priest, The Pleiades, night and Nuit among others.

25 is the number of Mars and the Star Ruby ritual.

- XX – V
- XIX – VI
- XVIII – VII
- XVII – VIII
- XVI – IX

North-East 231

This also includes three sides of the square. XXI to XVI is 111, a number of Aleph, which Crowley contrasts lightning (light) with the thick darkness and sudden death.

The South-East side sums to 45, which we have already seen as Adam and Yesod etc.

The paired cards sum to 15 the Mystic Number of Geburah
0 – XV I – XIV II – XIII III – XIV IV – XII V – X

SW-SE 231

The longest sequence presented here as 12 numbers, but if we unite XXI with XX then there are 11 pairs and includes another 31 (8 in all)

- XXI – X = 31
- 0 – XX = 20
- I – XIX
- II – XVIII
- III – XVII
- IV – XVI
- V – XV
- VI – XIV
- VII – XIII
- VIII – XII
- IX – XI

20 is the number of Kaph The Wheel, Yod The Hand of God, the letter of the Father, and KHR.

North 462

The top two sides sum to 462, the Supernal Earth, and a Path.

Square of Jupiter

Within the four sides is a square of Jupiter from which various sigils can be derived. Jupiter is of course Fortune, the Wheel, which suggests the squaring of the circle.

90

90 is explicit in the system as the angle of a square and quarter of a circle. According to Crowley, 90 is:

> 90 Number of Tzaddi, a fishhook = Tanha, the clinging of man to life (9), the trap in which man is caught as a fish is caught by a hook. The most

material aspect of animal life; its final doom decreed by its own lust. also MIM, Water.

In a commentary on *AL* II.77 Crowley says:

But 90 is Tzaddi, the 'Emperor', and 8, Cheth, the 'Charioteer' or Cup-Bearer; the phrase might them conceivably mean 'with majesty'.

KYYN as wine, DMM very silent, MLK Kings, MN manna. In Chapter 55 of the *Book of Lies* Crowley notes:

The number 90 is the last paragraph is not merely fact, but symbolism; 90 being the number of Tzaddi, the Star, looked at in its exoteric sense, as a naked woman, playing by a stream, surrounded by birds and butterflies. The pole-axe is recommended instead of the usual razor, as a more vigorous weapon. One cannot be too severe in checking any faltering in the work, any digression from the Path.

90 is YKYN, Jachin, Pillar.

Returning to the *Book of Lies*, Chapter 90, Starlight, concerns Laylah, Babalon, and Nuit. Crowley concludes with:

This chapter is a sort of final Confession of Faith. It is the unification of all symbols and all planes. The End is inexpressible.

ABRAHADABRA spread

Aleister Crowley includes the Society of Eight system of Tarot divination verbatim, but with some amendments as seen in *The Equinox*.

This system of divination is deliberately misleading for a number of reasons, one is the problem of dividing 78 into any meaningful groupings—it is impossible to have an equal number of cards in the stacks. Another problem is that as it stands, the stages do not represent Crowley's magical system. In *The Equinox*, Crowley hints as much. Balance is critical to magical workings.

Put simply, there is no viable magical system used by Crowley based upon the 12 signs of the Zodiac and of the Houses, while for the 36 Decanates, where to put the extra six cards? The final stage is also not balanced.

The First Operation is very useful—I use this professionally (see my earlier books). The Key to understanding this stage is to use the Formula of the Tetragrammaton discussed at length in the *Book of Thoth*. The fourth stack, of the Princesses or Disks, is from outside the system, translated into tarot speak, 'the future'. Crowley makes the point that prediction is based upon the random order of the cards, which is unsatisfactory. Put another way, the first three stacks are known to the querent, while the fourth stack is an unknown. This system is alchemical, and discussed in great depth by Carl Jung as a therapeutic technique.

Clues to the real system are found in the Society of Eight, and developed by Crowley. While I have focussed on importance of Eight as Mercury, Venus should not be underestimated. Venus is the Key as seen in the sigil of the A∴A∴ and in the diagram of the 'Days of the Week', page 11: the planets are primary.

The mathematics of 7 and 11 gives the system; 7 stacks of 11 cards, with one extra for the 'Significator'. This system is perfect for a number of reasons, and it is very powerful. The first question is in what order do we attribute the planets? Page 11 gives the Chaldean Order and the 'Days of the Week'—we have a choice. Crowley misattributes the diagram on page 11 as a Hexagram and Hexagon, which gives a clue to an alternative order, which is the Numbers of the Planets (page 275).

The versatility of this spread can be summarised as:

• Planetary squares
• Days of the Week
• The Sephiroth (p. 275)
• Chaldean Order

Irrespective of whether we lay out the cards in a Hexagram or Heptagram, there is always the Significator, which can be approached in two ways. Firstly, we can determine the nature of the question, determine the card that represents it, and lay this card separately, or we can trust to luck and discover the 78th card is after dealing out the stacks (this is essentially the bottom card which can be removed before dealing).

While 78 is the primary analysis of the *Book of Thoth*, 77 is a significant number:

> 77 OZ THE SUBLIME AND SUPREME SEPTENARY IN ITS MATURE MAGICAL MANIFESTATION THROUGH MATTER—AS IT IS WRITTEN—AN HE-GOAT ALSO.
>
> (Chapter 77, *Book of Lies*)

OZ, the Goat, scil. of the Sabbath of the Adepts. The Baphomet of the Templars, the idol set up to defy and overthrow the false god—though it is understood that he himself is false, not an end, but a means. Note the 77 = 7 × 11, magical power in perfection.

(Liber 58)

77 is BOH prayed, while MGDL means towers or citadels (Atu 16), so the spread can be seen as an invocation and protection, also as a means to break down a system or escape from past influences (Cephaloedium Working).

'Magical power in perfection' refers to ABRAHADABRA, a word of 11 letters, which Crowley analyses extensively, see 418 in 777. 418 is massively important for so many reasons, not least the number of Cheth, the Enochian Aethyrs, and the *Book of the Law*.

Incidentally, the lack of importance of the Zodiac and houses becomes clear with the card counting system for with this spread of 11 cards in a stack means that 12 always counts on to the originating card. This sense of unity in the signs of the Zodiac is found in *Liber 963*.

Each letter of ABRAHADABRA rule the position of each of the 11 cards in a stack, which makes for a convenient matrix or table of 7 × 11 for recording and subsequent detailed analysis.

By now it should be obvious why this system of Magick was hidden behind the five stages of the tarot spread. For this reason it is better to use only the first stage when reading for members of the public.

This spread, in whatever form and system used, is very intense, and should not be used for trivial reasons.

At the centre is HAD, whose number is 555, which is also the number of the Alephs in the name (111 × 5 = 555) and the number of *Liber HAD*. 555 appears in the Amalantrah Working, but in his analysis Crowley makes this number central to the Bornless Ritual.

The recurrence of 5 requires further thought. It is the number of Mars, Geburah, and Horus, while 55 is the Mystic Number of Malkuth, the Princess or Daughter redeemed in Binah. In one sense, although ABRAHADABRA is the means as 11, the result is 10 which takes us out of the system, see page 274.

Allied to 555 is V.V.V.V.V. (see Atu II).

Thus, the primary Atu for the ABRAHADABRA spread are: Atus 0, I, II, III to complete the Supernal Triangle.

As we can see, this spread is very powerful, not for dilettante or frivolous uses.

Methods of analysis

Analysis requires very high levels of knowledge of Crowley's system, so it is better to start with the First Operation, YHVH and then gradually work up to the ABRAHADABRA spread.

Card pairing

Within each stack there is card pairing which will always start on the first and last Aleph, and finish on the central Aleph. In other words, pairing with Aleph invokes HAD.

The second level of pairing is with BR/RB, 202 to make clean, elevate, empty, which refers to The Fool. Note the 202nd verse of *Liber AL* which also refers to The Fool. 202 is a metathesis of 220, the number of verses in *Liber AL*.

Combined we have 404 QDSh Holy, almond, and DTh Law, edict.

HD is 9, the number of Strong One, Brother AVB, fire, Obeah, and HAD itself.

HAD is 10, the influence from a strange source, the Daughter or Princess, which we see in Crowley's analysis of the Formula of the Tetragrammaton, which brings in the circular system.

In essence, HAD is twin, the name hidden at the centre with the quintessence of five Alephs.

Card counting

As mentioned previously counting 12 is redundant; landing on one of the 12 Atu terminates the count.

Card counting is performed within the stack, but there is another technique; counting the top cards which can be repeated ten times for the lower levels.

Regimen for divination

1. Invoke Tahuti twice daily.
2. Invocation of the Dawn Meditation daily.
3. Intensive study of the *Book of Thoth*, 777, and other books.
4. Regular use of the First Operation for clients until one becomes adept.
5. For Adepts: ABRAHADABRA spread.

CHAPTER TWENTY FOUR

The hidden influence of Allan Bennett

O f all the cryptic pages of the *Book of Thoth*, page 11 is one of the most enigmatic. Yet, Crowley gives clues that point to this page. What do we have? Three diagrams. Three suggests three Mother Letters, so there is clearly a link to the Sepher Yetsirah. The triangle is not obvious since the bottom diagram is horizontal which suggests the square or YHVH. Looked at another way, the top two diagrams portray a feminine yin line with third a yang line, a bigram in other words. The Mother Letters attributed to the diagrams give Air to the Unicursal Hexagram, Water to the 'Days of the Week', while Shin is for the signs of the Zodiac, which also covers the Double and Single letters of the Sepher Yetsirah. A pleasing symmetry. The Mother Letters also point to the Caduceus so prominent in the Appendices.

The gematria of the '8 Colour Plates' indicates the 'Days of the Week' mislabelled as Hexagram and Hexagram by Crowley, but of course the universal Hexagram also has six points. Six is a perfect number and apart from Sol also indicates the altar, which is constructed with two cubes—see what he did? The cube defines the six directions of space beloved of the author of the Sepher Yetsirah. If you ever wondered why Crowley does not discuss the Sepher Yetsirah, now you know it was there all the time.

Returning to 'The Theory of the Correspondences of the Tarot' we start with unity and love, AChD, AHBH = 13 which doubled gives 26 or YHVH. Allan Bennett's *A Note on Genesis* also starts with AChD and then moves on to *Genesis* I.1 which has seven words in Hebrew. Furthermore, the first word BRAShYTh has six letters, and considering that there are seven days of creation in Genesis makes us look again at the second diagram. Jumping to the Opening of the Key spread which Crowley presents almost verbatim, at the end he warns of the dangers of demonic or black magic influence and a Faustian pact, which is rather strange. He also points to the chapter in *Book IV* on The Moon, when it is clearly The Star that he is referring to.

Ignoring for the moment the number 5, the omission of that most sacred of numbers, 9, is astonishing, but fortunately Bennett comes to the rescue, for he says:

> *And finally the word HARTz, Ha Aretz, the Earth, hath four Letters showing its Elemental Constitution, and its Key is 17—also Hope—Hope in the Earth as there is Hope in Heaven. And the last letter of the verse is Tzaddi (the letter of Hope), by Qabalah of Nine Chambers that number which contains in itself all the properties of Protean Matters: howsoever you may multiply it the Key of its Numbers is ever 9. Fitting Symbol of ever-changing matter which ever in its essence is One—one and alone!*

Earth is the missing element in the Sepher Yetsirah, but Bennett binds it to YHVH and to The Star card and Tzaddi. Hardly a coincidence, but here is the kicker, *A Note on Genesis* was written in 1902, two years before the *Book of the Law*, and considering the importance Crowley places on Bennett's essay it is astonishing he omits to mention it when discussing the transposition of The Star with The Emperor, the 5th Atu. Just to tease everyone, the third diagram purports to show this transposition on the Zodiac with its twists.

It is the mystery that never was.

The number 10 is on the previous page, which has those four questions which Crowley conveniently replies to furnishing us with the richness of scrunch, so what might he have for us on page 12? He mentions a forgotten chess master, but he was probably thinking of that other forgotten master Eliphas Levi, who wrote in *The Key of the Mysteries*:

> *"The game of chess, attributed to Palamedes, has no other origin than the Tarot, and one finds there the same combinations and the same symbols:*

the king, the queen, the knight, the soldier, the fool, the tower, and houses
representing numbers. In old times, chess-players sought upon their chess-
board the solution of philosophical and religious problems, and argued
silently with each other in manoeuvring the hieroglyphic characters across
the numbers. Our vulgar game of goose, revived from the old Grecian game,
and also attributed to Palamedes, is nothing but a chess-board with motion-
less figures and numbers movable by means of dice. It is a Tarot disposed
in the form of a wheel, for the use of aspirants to initiation. Now, the word
Tarot, in which one finds 'rota,' and 'tora,' itself expresses, as William
Postel has demonstrated, this primitive disposition in the form of a wheel."

The use of dice is interesting, for it takes us back to six.
Levi goes on to say:

The hieroglyphs of the game of goose are simpler than those of the Tarot,
but one finds the same symbols in it: the juggler, the king, the queen, the
tower, the devil or Typhon, death, and so on. The dice-indicated chances of
the game represent those of life, and conceal a highly philosophical sense
sufficiently profound to make sages meditate, and simple enough to be
understood by children.

The allegorical personage Palamedes, is, however, identical with
Enoch, Hermes, and Cadmus, to whom various mythologies have attrib-
uted the invention of letters. But, in the conception of Homer, Palamedes,
the man who exposed the fraud of Ulysses and fell a victim to his revenge,
represents the initiator or the man of genius whose eternal destiny is to be
killed by those whom he initiates. The disciple does not become the living
realization of the thoughts of the Master until he had drunk his blood and
eaten his flesh, to use the energetic and allegorical expression of the initia-
tor, so ill understood by Christians.

Crowley may well have believed that this paragraph was written
expressly for him, reflecting his dealings with Mathers and the Golden
Dawn.

Palamedes is not so well known, but Levi feels the need to restate his
importance in similar fashion in High Magic:

... the first language being hieroglyphic and universal, a monument
of which has been preserved in the Book of Enoch, Cadmus, Thoth and
Palamedes, the kabalistic clavicle adopted later on by Solomon, the mys-
tical book of the TERAPHIM, URIM and THUMMIM, the primeval

Genesis of the Zohar and of William Postel, the mystical wheel of Ezekiel,
the ROTA of the Kabalists, the Tarot of Magi and Bohemians.

In November 1905 Crowley wrote *The High History of Good Sir Palamedes The Saracen Knight and of His Following of The Questing Beast* dedicated to Allan Bennett. The ROTA turns full circle.

CHAPTER TWENTY FIVE

TARO as a Map of the Universe

Contrary to everybody's impression, the Tarot Cards were not intended for the purposes of divination. They are a Map of the Universe.

(Frieda Harris)

In her lectures, Frieda Harris states that the TARO is a *Map of the Universe*. She also confirms that the tarot cards may be compared with the symbols of mathematics, i.e. constants. These constants are used in mathematical equations to solve problems, group and regroup forces and elements. Each card represents the play of opposites, active and passive, exemplified in Wheel—and Woah!

The models to be used in conjunction with the Taro are based on the mathematics of 8; the strategy of chess and the hexagrams of the I Ching for guidance on correct action. It is no coincidence that after meeting Frieda for the first time, Aleister made a concerted effort to perform a daily divination with the *I Ching* using the yarrow stalks that previously he had lost. Only severe ill-health prevented consultations, he even records the odd day where he forgot to consult the *I Ching*. Wherever possible he plays chess daily, but this depended on finding a willing opponent.

The Tarot, Chess, and *I Ching* form the perfect Vital Triad. The reason for the absence of divinatory meanings in the *Book of Thoth* is that in contrast to the constants of the cards, the meanings are variables dependent on circumstance. The meanings are Maya, Illusion and fall under the rulership of Atu I. Crowley gives divinatory meanings for the Major Arcana as *intent*, rather than for divination. *Map of the Universe* is a synonym for the Taro.

> The whole of 777 is an 'Encyclopaedia of the Holy Qabalah, which is a Map of the Universe, and enables man to attain Perfect Understanding'.
> This is the Constitution and Government of our Holy Order; by the study of its Balance you may yourself come to apprehension of how to rule your own life. For, in True Things, all are but images one of another; man is but a map of the universe, and Society is but the same on a larger scale.
> Liber CXCIV: An Intimation with Reference to the Constitution of the Order
> The [Geomantic] system is consequently based upon 16 figures and no more. Of course all systems of divinations which have any claim to be reasonable are based upon a map of the universe, or at least the Solar system, and 16 is really rather a limited number of units to manipulate.
> (*Magic without Tears*)

> There was a bad aspect to seven, because ten was the completion of the units, and a map of the universe having been constructed on the basis of these ten numbers, and the first three being given to the Trinity, the remaining seven were called the Inferiors. Thus in the Qabalah we have 'ten hells' grouped in seven palaces!
> (*Liber 888*)

An elaborate magical Map of the Universe on particular principles.

> Adonis an Allegory
> Lo! In the first of thine Initiations, when first the Hoodwink was uplifted from before thine Eyes, thou wast brought unto the Throne of Horus, the Lord of the Lion, and by Him enheartened against Fear. Moreover, in Minutum Mundum, the Map of the Universe, it is the Path of the Lion that bindeth the two Highest Faculties of thy Mind.
> (*Liber Aleph*)

There are three mentions of the *Map of the Universe* in the *Book of Thoth*:

1. The Tarot and the Holy Qabalah
2. The Naples Arrangement
3. The Twenty-Two Keys, Atu, or trumps of the Tarot

> *The Court Cards and small cards form the skeletal structure of the Tarot in its principal function as a Map of the Universe. But, for the special significance of the pack as a Key to magical formula, the 22 trumps acquire a peculiar importance.*
>
> *(Book of Thoth)*

The Latin phrase for *Map of the Universe* is the *Minutum Mundum*, which particularly refers to the colour scales and the Tetragrammaton. Crowley unites the Taro with the *Book of the Law* and Atu 0 in a remarkable passage:

> *I proclaim Blessing and Worship unto Nuith our Lady and her Lord, Hadith, for the Miracle of the Anatomy of the Child Ra-Hoor-Khuit, as it is shewed in the design Minutum Mundum, the Tree of Life. For though Wisdom be the Second Emanation of His Essence, there is a path to separate and to join them, the Reference thereof being Aleph, that is One indeed, but also an Hundred and Eleven in his full Orthography; to signify the Most Holy Trinity. And by metathesis it is Thick Darkness, and Sudden Death. This is also the Number of AUM, which is AMOUN, and the Root-Sound of OMNE or, in Greek, PAN; and it is a Number of the Sun. Yet is the Atu of Thoth that correspondeth thereunto marked with ZERO, and its Name is MAT, whereof I have spoken formerly, and its Image is The Fool. O, my son, gather thou all these Limbs together into one Body, and breathe upon it with thy Spirit, that it may live; then do thou embrace it with Lust of thy Manhood, and go in unto it, and know it; so shall ye be One Flesh. Now at last in the Reinforcement and Ecstasy of this Consummation thou shalt wit by what Inspiration thou didst choose thy Name in the Gnosis, I mean Parzival, 'der reine Thor', the True Knight that won Kingship in Monsalvat, and made whole the Wound of Amfortas, and ordered Kundry to Right Service, and regained the Lance, and revived the Miracle of the Sangraal; yea, also upon himself did he accomplish his Word in the end: 'Höchsten Heiles Wunder! Erlösung dem Erlöser!' This is the last*

Word of the Song that thine Uncle Richard Wagner made for Worship of this Mystery. Understand thou this, O my Son, as I take leave of thee in this Epistle, that the Summit of Wisdom is the Opening of the Way that leadeth unto the Crown and Essence of all, to the Soul of the Child Horus, the Lord of the Aeon. This is the Path of the pure fool.

(Liber Aleph)

No doubt Crowley was inspired in part by:

Concerning Minutum Mundum, we found it kept in another little Altar, truly more finer than can be imagined by any understanding man; but we will leave him undescribed, untill we shal truly be answered upon this our true hearted Famam; and so we have covered it again with the plates, and set the altar thereon, shut the door, and made it sure, with all our seals; besides by instruction and command of our Rota, there are come to sight some books, among which is contained M.

(Fama Fraternitas)

The *Minutum Mundum* plays an important part in the Vault of Initiation with the 'little altar' in the Rose Cross found on the back of the Taro cards.

Seven other Petals encircle these Three, each again shines forth in its true Colour, forming the Rainbow of Promise; but of Promise fulfilled, since the Circle is Complete. Upon each Petal appears another Sacred Letter, the Letters of the Seven Planets, those great Elementary Rulers whose Influence is ever-present and whose Aid and Co-operation of the Great Celestial Intelligences. Who, through thine own Holy Guardian Angel, are ever ready and willing to lend thee of their Wisdom and Power. These are the Rulers of the Sephiroth below Chokmah and above Malkuth, according to the Plan of the Minutum Mundum which thou saw'st upon the small altar within the Vault of Initiation.

(I.N.R.I. De Mysteriis Rosæ Rubeæ Et Aureæ Crucis by ONE whose Number is 777. (Frater AChD))

PART FIVE

CONCLUSIONS

CHAPTER TWENTY SIX

What is the *Book of Thoth?*

A leister Crowley went through hell managing the people and project on the astral planes as on the practical level. The energies unleashed through the work on the cards clashed with the magical wars raging to prevent the *Book of Thoth* ever seeing the light of day. Several times he nearly died. Fortunately Crowley guaranteed success with the powerful protective spirits from Abra-melin and Tahuti.

Writing and publishing a book is challenging at the best of times— Crowley was vastly experienced in the process—but the *Book of Thoth* was different. While the Atu in particular appear individually, explicitly or hidden, in so much of his writings, he had never wrote a book dedicated to the Taro where all 78 cards are addressed. The *Book of Thoth* is a collaboration with an artist who knew nothing of the tarot or magic, despite being a co-mason.

Frieda Harris was trained in the magical arts as expediently as possible. Little is known about the process of initiation she underwent in the A∴A∴, but we know the results. In a few years she became a magician versed in the arts of invocation, to Tahuti in particular.

Put another way, the *Book of Thoth* is a powerful grimoire created by two magicians who had to overcome the vicissitudes experienced in a country that lived in fear of invasion, wartime shortages and the threat of death. Crowley could have moved to a safer place in the countryside, but he chose to stay in London. Plans were made to decentralise the precious documents in case of a direct hit.

Magick is the *Book of Thoth*. Magick is Maya, Illusion—nothing is what it seems. Penetrating this Illusion is the duty of the tarot student.

There are many illusions to dispel; Not least of which, who Aleister Crowley really is. For the first year of trying to write this book I found myself confronted with every meme and trope perpetrated by himself on himself, as well as the common misperceptions and propaganda that we are all subjected to. My ideas about Crowley, his magic, his ideology, the tarot and the *Book of Thoth* changed on a daily basis. The journey was a constant flip-flop of discovery, rejection, and reintegration too tedious to record. I lost count of the number of times I started a statement with 'the *Book of Thoth* is ...', only for it to be contradicted hours or days later.

Writing a book is impossible under these conditions. Eventually I found myself focussing not on the cards, but on Part I: 'The Theory of the Tarot', where Crowley subverts what the reader thinks he knows on the subject. Superficially he is merely restating what we already know—and it is boring and tedious in places. Crowley does not do boring and tedious! Here is where the magick takes place. The student is taken from the darkness to the light, and he does not even know it is happening. Powerful dreams and visions inspired me to continue.

The chapters that have preceded represent core ideas in the *Book of Thoth* that became constants. Re-reading the manuscript six months later, I still agree with these views. In contrast, my views on the individual tarot cards remain fluid. What each card means depends on a long list of variables—the weather, knowledge of the reader, knowledge of the client, global politics, religious beliefs, magical beliefs, etc., etc.

The only way to view the cards is as mathematical terms or constants which are used in equations. Mathematicians invent new mathematical systems to solve problems. Cards can be grouped into classes, which for our purposes, are numbers, Hebrew alphabet, Zodiac signs, planets, elements, and so on. The equations are the tarot spreads, and here it gets interesting, for the system found on page 249 is deficient in a very obvious way. Crowley describes the system as 'The traditional technical method of divination' presented verbatim from *Book T*. The union of the magical formulae of ABRAHADABRA and BABALON is the missing tarot spread which unlocks the *Book of Thoth*.

While negotiating with publishers and completing the *Book of Thoth*, Aleister Crowley worked on these publications.

- *Temperance: A Tract for the Times*, 22 December 1939
- *Olla*, 1946
- *The I Ching* (incomplete)
- *Thumbs Up!*
- *Magick Without Tears*
- *Liber OZ*
- *The City of God: A Rhapsody*
- *Khing Khan King*
- *The Dangers of Mysticism*

APPENDIX

THE ORIGINAL COVER DESIGN OF THE BOOK OF THOTH

The design of the original cover of the *Book of Thoth* is not mere decoration, for it contains powerful secrets.

The Universe on the front cover

The front cover depicts Atu XXI, the final card of the Tarot, of which Aleister Crowley says:

> *In the present card she is represented as a dancing figure. In her hands she manipulates the radiant spiral force, the active and passive, each possessing its dual polarity. her dancing partner is shown as Heru-Ra-Ha of Atu XIX. 'The Sun, Strength & Sight, Light'; these are for the servants of the Star & the Snake. AL II.21 This final form of the image of the Magical Formula of the God combines and transforms so many symbols that description is difficult, and would be nugatory. The proper method of study of this card—indeed of all, but of this especially—is long-continued meditation. The Universe, so states the theme, is the **Celebration of the Great Work accomplished.***

Thoth on the back cover

Thoth invoking TARO

A line drawing by Frieda Harris. Thoth is holding in his right hand the Wand of the Chief Adept, similar to the sketch of Daniel in the *Cipher Manuscript*.

The palm of his left hand holds a bowl (laver of the seas?) upon which stands the Ankh of Venus or the Hanged Man. Thus, we have Mercury on the left and Venus on the right.

Around the Ankh are the letters TARO.

The four elements are:

- Wand – Fire
- Bowl – Water
- Ankh – Air
- TARO – Earth

Combined, they form Spirit. The legs of Thoth show forward movement, as in TO GO.

Thoth invoking

INVOCATION

Any desired Tarot Card can be invoked in this way by begetting its hierarchy, and giving them our own bodies to manifest through, by feeding (feeling) the Eucharist.

(Amalantrah Working)

Take the cards in your left hand. In the right hand hold the wand over them, and say:

I invoke thee, I A O, that thou wilt send H R U, the great Angel that is set over the operations of this Secret Wisdom, to lay his hand invisibly upon these consecrated cards of art, that thereby we may obtain true knowledge of hidden things, to the glory of thine ineffable Name. Amen.

Aiwaz! confirm my troth with Thee! my will inspire
With secret sperm of subtle, free, creating Fire!
Mould thou my very flesh as Thine, renew my birth
In childhood merry as divine, enchanted Earth!
Dissolve my rapture in Thine own, a sacred slaughter
Whereby to capture and atone the Soul of Water!
Fill thou my mind with gleaming Thought intense and rare

213

To One refined, outflung to naught, the Word of Air!
Most, bridal bound, my quintessential Form thus freeing
From self, be found one Selfhood blent in Spirit-Being.

Then quote the relevant verse from the Book of Thoth for the specific Tarot card.

INVOCATION AND MAGICK VIA
THE PRINCESSES

The leitmotif of the *Book of Thoth* concerns the Princess who comes from a strange quarter bringing news. Just what that news might be is for the student to discover. Beyond the obvious textual structure of sections and chapters of the *Book of Thoth* runs a Qabalistic system based upon YHVH. The Princess is the final H, the Daughter, who is also represented as Malkuth, The Gate appended to, and separate from the bottom of the Qabalistic Tree of Life.

In the occult world secret knowledge is a cliché, which rapidly degenerates into what magicians *think* is secret knowledge that only they know. Occult organisations are no different. Crowley had first-hand experience of just how badly and quickly everything can go pear-shaped, the consequences of which reverberate to this day, not that anyone cares. Crowley's over-riding desire was to meet the Secret Masters; he was lead to the right people in the wrong group who had the means to meet the Secret Masters, but they abused the system.

Then there are those groups who believed they owned Crowley, but he was merely fulfilling his fraternal obligation to help his brothers, of whatever Order. Looking at the current shambolic state of these organisations, they badly need another Aleister Crowley today.

It was his solitary expeditions, particularly to Mexico where he invented his own system based upon Eliphas Levi and the Society of Eight. Later, he met another maverick, John Yarker, a member of the now defunct Society of Eight, and together they secretly re-established the system in plain view.

Despite his best efforts, Crowley never found a worthy successor. There were candidates, but they all failed the tests. As we know, the best candidates are those who have no interest in the power politics, unencumbered with rigid ideological beliefs antithetical to Crowley's grand design of making the Secret Chiefs available to all those who desire.

The ideologically blinkered ignore the multiplicity of hints to solve the puzzle, while doing everything in their power to prevent others find the Light. In this respect they are the inheritors of the Black Brothers.

While studying Crowley's writings in the light of his true intentions, I am continually amazed at his endurance, patience, and ingenuity. He has style. Meanwhile there is the ongoing agenda of positing a minor aberration at the end of his life where he lost the plot due to the machinations of Frieda Harris in a crude attempt to disparage both. Maybe the reason for these continual character assassinations is that they too know the truth and they know they are running out of time.

QUOTATIONS

Expressing the Tarot in simplistic terms will always miss the point. There is no beginning nor end to the Wheel—where does one start? When does it end? By its nature, any discourse on the Wheel will bring us back to same point, but not necessarily at the same time and place. Aleister Crowley weaves in many narratives that often intersect causing inevitable repetition. The formation of some of his ideas and the creation of the tarot involved the interaction of notable people in his life.

When Aleister met Frieda

Meum Stewart and Leslie Blanche, that brilliant artist, told me that their education was far from finished until they met the Worst Man in the World: so, naturally, I invited him and them to dinner, at the Royal Automobile Club. At the last moment, as it were, Lady Harris *joined us. In order to excite Crowley, I introduce Mrs Blanche as 'la Comtesse de Roussy de Sales', but he was not deceived, and out of that meeting came the fine collaboration in The Tarot Cards, of Crowley and Lady Harris.*

(Clifford Bax from *Some I Knew Well*, 1951)

Playwright Clifford Bax (1886–1962) is a long-time friend of Aleister Crowley—they were playing chess together in 1904. He also introduced John Symonds to Crowley, helped Allan Bennett with his writings, and edited *Golden Hind* by Austin Osman Spare.

Frieda's impressions of the Book of Thoth

As the artist and confidante of Aleister Crowley, Frieda Harris was uniquely placed to synthesise her experiences of painting the cards under the guidance of Tahuti. She describes the cosmic powers and forces at work, and the uses of the cards beyond mere divination.

> *Contrary to everybody's impression, the Tarot Cards were not intended for the purposes of divination. They are a Map of the Universe and they might quite easily be compared with the symbols of mathematics. Regarded as such they represent a convenient means of stating cosmic problems, such as the grouping and regrouping of forces, elements and so on, which have in the last accounted for the course taken by history of the universe and they will probably continue to shape it in the future.*
>
> *Like mathematics too that admit of numerous different interpretations and just as there have been different forms of mathematical thinking, so the designs used for the Tarot Cards have differed greatly through the ages. In fact the difference between Euclid and Einstein are not greater than the differences between any two sets of Tarot Cards. These packs of Tarot cards have been described as the Tarot of the Egyptians and the Bohemians, in other words the Gypsies.*
>
> (Frieda Harris Lecture, 1942)

> *The Tarot could be described as God's Picture Book or it could be likened to a celestial game of chess, the Trumps being the pieces to be moved according to the law of their own order over a chequered board of the four elements.*
>
> *The legend runs that the Adepts in the Sanctuary of the Gnosis at the time of the Christian Era that the Adepts being anxious to conceal their heretical doctrines from the extravert Christian teaching, decided to put their secrets in the form of a game of cards to be seen by all and understood by few. In many cases the letters and signs attributed to the Trumps have been willfully interchanged to confuse the true meaning.*
>
> *Each of the ideas embodied in these pictures seems in space, so that you can approach them from many different aspects such as Alchemy,*

*Symbolism, Science, Geometry, whatever your favourite kick-off is, and
you will probably find out that the conclusions would bring you out in the
words of Omar Kyam at the same door wherein you went, but you will also
have sensed the feeling of movement and rhythm proper to elemental forces
which is implicit in the Tarot.*

*This tidal movement adds to the difficulty of defining the cards, but as
I painted them I did get some idea of forces beyond the control of human
intellect, the relentless procedure of a cosmic plan, the inevitability of the
solution of every problem, and the necessity of finding this solution, not in
personal emotion but in controlling law—which I believe is the right use
of the Tarot.*

(Frieda Harris Lecture, 1944)

Spinning the wheel

TARO, ROTA, TORA, and ATOR are interchangeable, but of course
there are nuances and applications to each. There is fluidity in the *Book
of Thoth* in spelling which can be confusing. When performing readings,
Crowley would often refer to the 'rota' rather than taro. TORA and
ATOR are rare forms. TORA is the Torah, the *Book of the Law*, while
ATOR is Hathor, the Empress and High Priestess.

Est fuga, volvitur rota (Metamorphoses) 'The spinning wheel lifts one
to Heaven' is cited by Robert Browning in *Master Hughes of Saxe-Gotha*
and in *Tannhäuser* by Aleister Crowley.

ROTA

The Word of The Equinox

In 1907 Aleister Crowley began issuing a word or phrase at each
Equinox. In Freemasonry the password for each Lodge would be
changed at the Equinox, so Crowley is continuing a venerable tradition.

Crowley used several methods, including bibliomancy on the Book
of the Law, seeing where his ring landed on a page at random, and often
a Hexagram from the *I Ching* by way of some explanation. Some of the
words were from Enochian magic, some from Abra-melin, and some
were invented, the meanings of which were not always clear, even
to Crowley.

The Word of the Equinox for Autumn 1940 was "R.O.T.A." formally
marking the beginning of the *Book of Thoth*. See the Title Page, where

we learn that the *Book of Thoth* is part of *The Equinox* series of books, Volume III No. V.

At the bottom of the Title Page we see that the *Book of Thoth* was formally published at the Spring Equinox of 1944 at 5:19 pm. Crowley would have created an electional horoscope to determine the optimal time, and he would have performed a magickal act culminating for that moment.

As we know, a limited edition of 200 signed copies were distributed around June of 1944.

Crowley often associated a Hexagram from the *I Ching*. For the Equinox of Autumn 1940 the associated Hexagram Wu Wang no. 25, Lingam of Fire is inspirational and prescient for Crowley to continue despite the many health problems he suffered at that time.

> *Sincerity and prudence; splendid*
> *if in these matters thou hast not offended.*
> *Free from all insincerity, press on!*
> *Good going, if thou reap with never a plough!*
> *Yet—innocence oft bears guilt's branded brow.*
> *Firmness, correctness; these bid woe begone.*
> *The good man sick? He needs no doctor-don.*
> *Time's come when silence's book is best to con.*

The oath of silence

Early in his career, Aleister Crowley took a solemn 'Oath of Silence about the Tarot', which should restrain him from speaking openly. Yet, his writings are imbued with tarot references. Such an oath becomes necessary when, as Agrippa observes:

> *Orpheus also, with a certain terrible authority of religion, did exact an oath of silence from those he initiated to the ceremonies of holy things.*

Fortunately, we know precisely what this Silence signifies, as elucidated on page 120 (take note of the number!), in an excerpt from *Little Essays Toward Truth*.

BOOK OF THOTH TIMELINE

1861
Kenneth Mackenzie visits Eliphas Levi in Paris to discuss the Tarot. They agree to publish a book on the subject. The account of this visit is published in *Rosicrucian and Red Cross* (1873).

1874
F.G. Irwin meets Eliphas Levi.

1875
Kenneth Mackenzie produces a prospectus for *The Game of Tarot*. Eliphas Levi dies.
Aleister Crowley born.

1882
Mathers and Frederick Holland join the SRIA.

1883
Frederick Holland forms the Society of Eight.

Frederick Holland letter to John Yarker on 31 July 1883:

> *a Society of Work, with a sincere end, and that end the sincere study of God & Nature—the result of which is undoubtedly the Stone—& Universal Medicine*

Mackenzie letter to F.G. Irwin on 28 August 1883:

> *I am glad to welcome you as a Brother of the Society of Eight—this Society means work and not play. It is by no means poor R.W. Little's foolish Rosicrucian Society. We are practical and not visionary and we are not degree-mongers. That nonsense is played out.*

Around this time *Book T* and the *Cipher Manuscript* are written based upon writings of Eliphas Levi.

1886
Kenneth Mackenzie dies.
Wynn Westcott and MacGregor Mathers obtain *Book T* and the *Cipher Manuscript* from Mackenzie's widow.

1887
1 October 1887: Wynn Westcott writes to Fräulein Sprengel.

1888
Hermetic Order of the Golden Dawn formed by MacGregor Mathers, Wynn Westcott, and Dr Woodman.

1892
Wynn Westcott publishes his translation of *The Magical Ritual of the Sanctum Regnum* by Eliphas Levi.

1894
Mathers is busy recruiting candidates into his Golden Dawn.
The Book of Splendors by Eliphas Levi published posthumously.
Allan Bennett joins the GD.
Aleister Crowley starts mountaineering.

1895
Major Keys and Minor Keys of Solomon by Eliphas Levi published.

1896
Wynn Westcott resigns from the Golden Dawn.
A.E. Waite re-joins the Inner Order of the Golden Dawn.
Mathers requires loyalty test from members.

1898
18 November 1898: Aleister Crowley initiated into the Golden Dawn as Neophyte.

1899
A.E. Waite enters the Second Order of the Golden Dawn.
W.B. Yeats attacks Aleister Crowley on the astral plane.

1900
Crowley attains Adeptus Minor 16 January.
Mathers alleges to Florence Farr that Wynn Westcott falsified the Frau Sprengel letters.
MacGregor Mathers and Aleister Crowley expelled from the GD.
Aleister Crowley travels to Mexico, receives the 33° from Don Jesus Medina.
Aleister Crowley forms his first temple, The Order of *LIL*.

1904
Aleister Crowley travels to Cairo, receives *Liber AL*, a ritual to break from Mathers' Golden Dawn and to create a new Order.
The *Sword of Song* published.

1907
A∴A∴ formed with George Cecil Jones.
Liber 231 written.
The *Wake World* published.

1908
Crowley writes to Wynn Westcott on the *Cipher Manuscripts*.

1909
Crowley publishes first volumes of *The Equinox*.
Liber AL is rediscovered in Boleskine.
Crowley and Victor Neuberg visit Tunisia to explore the Enochian Aethyrs.

1910
Mathers sues Crowley on GD ritual copywrite.
Westcott discovers the slanders made against him by Mathers in the GD in 1900.
Aleister Crowley invokes Mars (Mars dominates MacGregor Mathers).
Book IV, Part 1 published.
Crowley achieves grade of Magister Templi.

1911
Liber 418 published.

1912
Crowley meets John Yarker and the pair collaborate.
O.TO. chartered by Yarker.
Sepher Sephiroth published.

1913
The *Book of Lies* published.
M.M.M. established.
John Yarker dies.

1914
Crowley travels to the US. Starts invoking Mercury daily.

1915
Crowley achieves grade of Magus.

1918
Amalantrah Workings commence.

1920
Crowley arrives at Cefalù.
Book IV completed.
Crowley starts writing The *Book of Thoth*.

1923
Crowley expelled from Italy.

1925

The *Heart of the Master* published (in German). Contains verses from the *Book of Thoth*.

1937

Aleister Crowley meets Frieda Harris. Crowley finds his lost yarrow stalks and starts working on the *I Ching*, and recording each divination every day.

Crowley makes final edits to the *Heart of the Master*.

1938

The *Heart of the Master* published in English.

Little Essays Toward Truth published.

1939

Eight Lectures on Yoga published.

Khing Kang King published. Frieda Harris receives copy no. 3.

England Stand Fast! published.

Temperance: A Tract for the Times published.

1940

Crowley works on *I Ching* book (incomplete and unpublished).

1941

The *Dangers of Mysticism* published.

Thumbs Up! published.

Liber OZ published.

The Fun of the Fair published.

1943

Magick Without Tears completed but not published until 1954.

1944

The *Book of Thoth* is published in a limited edition of 200 copies.

1946

Olla published.

SELECTED BIBLIOGRAPHY

Cipher Manuscript (circa 1880) Society of Eight working document focussing on Ritual and the Atu. This document was used by Mathers to formulate the Golden Dawn system.

Book T (circa 1880) Society of Eight working document on the Minor Arcana, the Court Cards and a system of divination. See *The Equinox*.

These two books dovetail together and have a common source in Eliphas Levi.

The Goetia By Macgregor Mathers

The Sacred Magic of Abra-melin (1889) Translation by MacGregor Mathers,

Liber 220 (1904) The *Book of the Law*

The Sword of Song (1904)

Konx Om Pax (1907)

Liber 418 (1911) Excerpts and references in *Book of Thoth* (see Appendix)

The Equinox (1909–1913) Volume 7 and 8 include the story of the Tarot as it relates to the GD. All the important books are found in their original form in The Equinox including *Liber AL vel Legis, 777, Liber 418, Liber 231,* etc. The full set of 10 facsimile volumes is an excellent investment.

Book of Lies (1913) Complementary to the tarot.

Book of Thoth (1920) Written at the same time as *Book IV* and updated while Frieda Harris painted the cards.

Book IV, **Part III** (1929) More on the Atu

Heart of the Master (1938) Originally published in German (1925) and then in English in 1938. The Heart of the Master includes the verses and divinatory meanings of the Atu.

Book of Thoth (1944)

Other books on Crowley

Grant & Symonds *Confessions of Aleister Crowley*

Grant & Symonds *The Magickal Diary of the Beast 666*

Harrison, D *The Life and Death of John Yarker*

Whitehouse, D **The Lady and the Beast: The Extraordinary Partnership between Frieda Harris and Aleister Crowley** 2025

Some books that influenced Aleister Crowley

Anon. The Holy Bible (KJV)

Anon. *Cipher Manuscript*

Anon. *Book T*

Burgoyne, T. *The Light of Egypt*

Frazier, J.G. *The Golden Bough*

Levi, E. *Dogme et Rituel de la Haute Magic Part II*

Levi, E. *The Magic Ritual of the Sanctum Regnum* translated by Wynn Westcott

Levi, E. *The Mysteries of the Qabalah*

Levi, E. *Book of Splendours*

Mathers. *Lesser Key of Solomon*

Mathers. *The Key of Solomon the King*

O'Neill, John. *The Night of the Gods*

Ragon, J. (1844) *The Mass and its Mysteries Compared to the Ancient Mysteries*

Skeat, W. *An Etymological Dictionary of the English Language*

Stirling, W. *The Canon—An Exposition of the Pagan Mystery perpetuated in the Cabala as the Rule of All Arts*

Sullivan, J.W.N. *Bases of Modern Science*

von Worms, Abraham. *The Book of the Sacred Magic of Abra-melin the Mage*

Yarker, J. (1910) *Arcane Schools*

Yarker, J. *Recapitulation of All Masonry*

Yarker, J. *Lectures of the Ancient and Primitive Rite of Freemasonry*

THE SECRET FORMULAE OF THE NEW AEON

Inspired by the reception of the *Book of the Law* in 1904, Aleister Crowley was busy with George Cecil Jones (Fr D.D.S.) working on the Great Work with his Augoeides, the method is 'invoke often', signified by A∴ in his writings. Naturally they were working with the spirits of Abra-melin.

On 27 July 1907 Crowley records this remarkable account.

> *Fra. P. was crucified by Fra. D.D.S. and on that cross made to repeat this oath: 'I, P——, a member of the Body of Christ, do hereby solemnly obligate myself, etc., to lead a pure and unselfish life, and will entirely devote myself so to raise, etc., myself to the knowledge of my higher and Divine Genius that I shall be He'.*
>
> *'In witness of which I invoke the great Angel Hua to give me a proof of his existence'.*
>
> *P. transcribe this, and continues: 'Complete and perfect visualization of ...' here are hieroglyphics which may mean 'Christ as P—on cross'. He goes on: 'The low dark hill, the storm, the star'. But the Pylon of the Camel (i.e. the path of Gimel) open, and a ray therein: withal a certain vision of A∴ remembered only as a glory now attainable.*

HUA is part of the solemn Obligation to one's HGA made at the Temple of *LIL*.

> *In my bondage and affliction, O Lord, let me raise Thy Holy Symbol alike of Suffering and of Strength. I invoke Thee, the great avenging angel HUA, to place thine hand invisibly upon mine head, in attestation of this mine Obligation!*

As a result of renewing the Obligation, on 9 August Crowley wrote the *Invocation of the Ring*, 'that is, of the symbolical episcopal ring of Amethyst, which I wore as an Exempt Adept'.

Crowley says:

> *I intended to use this Invocation in practice. The amethyst was to be, so to speak, the lens through which the Holy Guardian Angel should manifest ... On the ninth, having prepared a full invocation and ritual, I performed it. I had no expectation, I think, of attaining any special success; but it came. I had performed the Operation of the Sacred Magick of Abra-Melin the Mage.*
>
> *It is unlawful to speak of the supreme sacrament. It was such, as the following entry shows, that I found it hard to believe that I had been permitted to partake of it. I will confine myself to the description of some of the ancillary phenomena.*

Crowley includes this invocation in *The Wake World* but with significant changes to the fourth verse.

Original	The Wake World
ADONAI! Thou inmost Fire,	ADONAI! Thou inmost Δ,
Self-glittering image of my soul,	Self-glittering image of my soul
Strong lover to thy Bride's desire,	Strong lover to thy Bride's desire,
Call me and claim me and control!	Call me and claim me and control!
I pray thee keep the holy tryst.	I pray Thee keep the holy tryst
Within this ring of Amethyst.	Within this ring of Amethyst

For on mine eyes the golden Sun / For on mine eyes the golden ☉

Hath dawned; my vigil slew the / Hath dawned; my vigil slew the

   Night. /   Night.

I saw the image of the One: / I saw the image of the One;

I came from darkness into Light. / I came from darkness into LVX

I pray Thee keep the holy tryst / I pray Thee keep the holy tryst

Within this ring of Amethyst. / Within this ring of Amethyst

INRI – me crucified, / I.N.R.I. – me crucified,

Me slain, interred, arisen, inspire! / Me slain, interred, arisen, inspire

T.A.R.O. – me glorified, / T.A.R.O. – me glorified,

Anointed, fill with frenzied Fire! / Anointed, fill with frenzied Δ!

I pray Thee keep the holy tryst / I pray Thee keep the holy tryst

Within this ring of Amethyst. / Within this ring of Amethyst

I eat my flesh: I drink my blood: / I eat my flesh: I drink my blood

I gird my loins: I journey far: / I gird my loins: I journey far:

For Thou hast shown the Rose, / For thou hast shown ○, +,

   the Rood,

The Eye, the Sword, the Silver Star. / ע, 777, καμήλον,

I pray thee keep the holy tryst / I pray Thee keep the holy tryst

Within this ring of Amethyst. / Within this ring of Amethyst

Prostrate I wait upon thy will, / Prostrate I wait upon thy will,

Mine Angel, for this grace of union. / Mine Angel, for this grace of union.

O let this Sacrament distil / O let this Sacrament distil

Thy conversation and communion. / Thy conversation and communion.

I pray Thee keep the holy tryst / I pray Thee keep the holy tryst

Within this ring of Amethyst. / Within this ring of Amethyst.

The ring is onomatopoeic, the sound invokes Akasha in silence—Spirit. The sound is made by a bell to summon the spirit (67, Zain a sword, and Binah, also silent). RING is a Tetragrammaton, 263, the number of gematria and Barkiel, the geomantic intelligence of Scorpio which fits in with the martial energy invoked. Reduced 263 is the number of magick, 11.

RING is Atus XIX, IX, XIII and II. Sun and Moon are united by the central letters. I is Yod, The Hermit, Yod is the 10th letter, the *phallus* and *kteis*, while YVD is 26, YHVH. IX is the Sacred Number Nine. Atu X is Fortune, letter Kaph, also *phallus* and *kteis*. 10 is X, the Cross, the place of crucifixion. The RING is therefore the Chemical Wedding of Christian Rosenkreuz. The RING as O is Atu XV The Devil.

Stanza 1 invokes Adonai as inner fire (Kether) identified with the soul of magician who unites with the Bride in Malkuth, the Princess of Disks. 'Strong' identifies with Lust. Line 4 is a remarkable plea for surrender, the Hanged Man. Line 5 is an entreaty to keep the promise of union. Line 6 establishes the place of the work in the Ring of Jupiter, KHR or Chesed. Lines 5 and 6 complete each of the five stanzas which form the Blazing Star (page 275).

Stanza 2 brings illumination from darkness to the light. The symbol of the Sun is also of Nuit and Hadit. The image of lines 1–4 is reminiscent of the 0° = 0° Neophyte Ritual.

Stanza 3 is the death and rebirth of the adept mirrored in the crucifixion and resurrection of Jesus Christ. ADNY is transfigured into T.A.R.O via I.N.R.I., and the Fire transforms into Spirit, Atu XX, or the Holy Ghost who anoints the adept. 'Frenzied' denotes the sexual union of Babalon and the Beast.

Stanza 4. Inspired by the inner fire of the Holy Ghost the adept commences his journey of transformation and transfiguration, figuratively and literally. The adept is shewn the symbols of power. In both versions the number of symbols is five, Geburah.

The Rose is a symbol of purity, love and mysticism. Rosicrucianism. The rose is feminine, another circle, which unites with the Rood, the phallus. The symbol used is the cross, the *Minutum Mundum*. The rose cross unites to form the Ankh (Atu XII), a form of which appears on the back of the tarot cards.

The Eye is Ayin, Atu XV, the Mountain of Abiegnus, the hidden fire. See the Princess of Disks.

The Sword is ZYN, 67, a number of Binah and of the Lovers. See the Ace of Swords. Upon the blade inscribe the Word to invoke. See 777 below.

The Priestess of the Silver Star is the High Priestess who stands over the members of the A∴A∴. καμῆλον is the Camel, symbol of the High Priestess whose Path ascends from Tipareth to Kether, uniting the previous verses.

777 is the World of Shells, i.e. the Qlippoth, and it is also 'One is the Spirit of the Living God'.

Aleister Crowley comments on this sacred number, the triple 7, whose sum is 21 AHYH and the number of the Atu in Roman Letters.

> *The Flaming Sword, if the path from Binah to Chesed be taken as = 3. For Gimel connects Arikh Anpin with Zauir Anpin.*
>
> *Useful in a similar way, as affirming that the Unity is the Qliphoth. But a dangerous tool, especially as it represents the flaming sword that drove Man out of Eden. A burnt child dreads the fire. 'The devils also believe, and tremble'. Worse than useless unless you have it by the hilt. Also 777 is the grand scale of 7, and this is useless to anyone who has not yet awakened the Kundalini, the female magical soul. Note 7 as the meeting-place of 3, the Mother, and 10, the Daughter; whence Netzach is the Woman, married but no more.*

Stanza 5. Prostrate in silent supplication, waiting for a sign of success and completion. The Will is of Adonai. The second line refers to line 1 of the previous verse.

Sacrament—Eliphas Levi says:

> *Its name Tarot suggests a connection with Tora, 'the sacramental name which the Jews give to their inspired book'. Its twenty-two trump cards recall the twenty-two letters of the Hebrew Alphabet, the twenty-two chapters of the mystical book of the Apocalypse, etc. In the sixteenth century William Postel, the Kabbalist, in his Clavis Absconditorum d Constitutione Mundi, inscribes on the circlet of his symbolic key the four letters TARO, but arranged in such a manner that it is uncertain how they should be read, and he writes of a hieroglyphic book which he calls the Genesis of Henoch. Finally, Eliphas Levi solemnly testifies:*
>
> *1. That without the Tarot the magic of the ancients is a sealed book.*
> *2. That it alone gives the true interpretation of the magic squares of the planetary genii as they are represented by Paracelsus.*

3. That the rabbinical notary art is at bottom nothing else but the science of the Tarot signs, and their complex and various application to the divination of all secrets.

4. That he himself has opened all the doors of the ancient sanctuaries and ascertained the significance of all symbols by the means of this instrument

(Eliphas Levi, *Mysteries of Magic*)

The 'planetary genii' of Paracelsus inspires Abra-melin.

See also *The Sevenfold Sacrament* by Aleister Crowley. In sex magick, the sacrament is the union of masculine and feminine fluids after orgasm.

Lines 3 and 4 signify the sacrament as the means to the Knowledge and Conversation with one's Holy Guardian Angel.

The Wheel of Tarot

The *Book of Thoth* opens with Chapter 78 of The *Book of Lies* (1913). Here is one interpretation of this text using simple gematria on English letters transposed into Hebrew.

Wheel and—Whoa!

The Great Wheel of Samsara.
The Wheel of the Law (Dhamma).
The Wheel of the Taro.
The Wheel of the Heavens.
The Wheel of Life.
All these Wheels be one; yet of all these the Wheel of the TARO alone avails thee consciously.
Meditate long and broad and deep, O man, upon this Wheel, revolving it in thy mind
Be this thy task, to see how each card springs necessarily from each other card, even in due order from The Fool unto The Ten of Coins.
Then, when thou know'st the Wheel of Destiny complete, mayst thou perceive THAT Will which moved it first. (There is no first or last.)
And lo! thou art past through the Abyss.

Wheel

51, Atu XII Initiation and Atu 0. '51 AN, pain. NA, failure. ADVM, Edom, the country of the demon kings. There is much in the Qabalah about these kings and their dukes; it never meant much to me, somehow. But 51 is 1 short of 52'.

and

'and' 55, the Mystic Number of Malkuth, which is reflexive, since 5+5 = 10. Also DVMH silence, Dagdagiel. AND is Initiation between The Fool and The Empress

– Whoa!

WOA! In the original title is 78. 77 without the exclamation mark is 'OZ, the Goat, scil. of the Sabbath of the Adepts. The Baphomet of the Templars, the idol set up to defy and overthrow the false god – though it is understood that he himself is false, not an end, but a means. Note the 77 = 7×11, magical power in perfection. 77 is GOD, also DOG'. The inclusion of H in Hebrew is 83, a prime number, 'Consecration: love in its highest form: energy, freedom, amrita, aspiration. The root of the idea of romance plus religion'. and a form of Gimel (Atu II). H in Greek is 8, making 86. Of this number Crowley says '86 ALHIM. See "A Note on Genesis", Equinox II'. and '86 Elohim, the original mischief. But good, since it is a Key of the Pentagram, 5 = 1 + 4–14 – 8 + 6 = 86'. The Pentagram is known as the Blazing Star in Freemasonry.

Taking the first letters of the title we have VAV, a nail (Atu V) which unites. VAV = 13 Love or Unity.

'Wheel and Whoa!' is the perfect expression of the duality of movement and change or the flow of time with stability, constancy or timelessness. In other words, the Ying and Yang of the Tao. The title therefore transforms into a trigram. Furthermore Vau means 'and' which renders the title as 18 ChY '18 ChY, Life. An "elaboration" of 9'. Expanded, 165 '11 x XV should be a number Capricorni Pneumatici. Not yet fulfilled'

The Great Wheel

See 20 KHR Liber 418

of Samsara.
Samsara, the wheel of rebirth and illusion. Identified with Fortune. Crowley identifies this as the Buddhist 'samsara cakkram' with 100 and 400, Qoph and Tau respectively. See also Liber 58 and Liber Porta Lucis.

The Wheel of the Law
Wheel of Law. See An Essay in Ontology, Berashith, Liber 71 and The Sword of Song. Also a reference to the Book of the Law (Liber 220) as a circle and Atu X

(Dhamma).
Dhamma. See Liber Aleph, An Essay in Ontology, Berashith, Liber 58, Liber 65, Liber 71, The Sword of Song. Also 'The Culture of the Mind' by Allan Bennett and the Dhammapada.
'We here purposely avoid dwelling on the mere silliness of many gematria correspondences, e.g. the equality of the Qliphoth of one sign with the Intelligence of another. Such misses are more frequent than such hits as AChD, Unity, 13 = AHBH, Love, 13. The argument is an argument in a circle. "Only an adept can understand the Qabalah", just as (in Buddhism) Sakyamuni said, "Only an Arahat can understand the Dhamma"'. The Temple of Solomon Part 5.

The Wheel of the Taro.
The Wheel of the Heavens.
Genesis I.1 ShMYM is Heavens, or 'The Names', i.e. the Divided Name of YHVH, the Shemhamphorash. ShMYM is 390, literally Fire and Water, 390, 39×2 = 78. Alternatively 390 is Shin (Atu 0 and Atu XX) and Atu XVII.

The Wheel of Life.
Another reference to Fortune.

All these Wheels be one; yet of all these the Wheel of the TARO
Repetition of 'Wheel of the Taro', but now the emphasis is on the united aspect of all these wheels.
alone avails thee consciously.
Meditate long and broad and deep, O man,

O man = Nemo, Master of the Temple. See Ab-ul-Diz, Aethyrs
2 ARN and 13 ZIM, Hymns to the Star Goddess, Confessions of
Aleister Crowley, Liber 220 I.33 commentary

upon this
  Wheel
  Eight Wheels in total,

revolving it in thy mind
  Be this thy task, to see how each card springs
  necessarily from each other card, even in due
  order from The Fool unto The Ten of Coins.
  Then, when thou know'st the Wheel of Destiny
  Wheel of Destiny: John St. John 'An Ixion bound to the Wheel
of Destiny and of the samsara, unable to reach the centre, where is
Rest'.

complete, mayst thou perceive THAT Will which
  moved it first. (There is no first or last.)
  And lo!
  Lo! LO = 100, Atu XVIII. With the exclamation mark 101 is 'JOY,
the Egg of Spirit in equilibrium between the Pillars of the Temple.
(Jachin and Boaz)' See The Dragon-Flies, Chapter 12 of the Book of
Lies.

thou art past through the Abyss.
  The TARO is the means for crossing the Abyss. See Atu II. See
Fortune, Atu X below.

                                        (Chapter 78, *Book of Lies*)

The Invocation of the Ring, Wheel, and—Whoa! Unite in the *Oath written
during the Dawn Meditation.* This Triad forms the secret Formulae for the
New Aeon fulfilled in the 22 Atu.

An Oath

Aiwaz! confirm my troth with Thee! my will inspire
With secret sperm of subtle, free, creating Fire!
Mould thou my very flesh as Thine, renew my birth
In childhood merry as divine, enchanted Earth!
Dissolve my rapture in Thine own, a sacred slaughter
Whereby to capture and atone the Soul of Water!
Fill thou my mind with gleaming Thought intense and rare
To One refined, outflung to naught, the Word of Air!
Most, bridal bound, my quintessential Form thus freeing
From self, be found one Selfhood blent in Spirit-Being.

(*Book of Thoth*, 1944; and *Olla*, 1946)

ABOUT THE AUTHOR

Paul Hughes-Barlow is a professional tarot reader since 1990. He studied with Punditt Maharaj, from a family of astrologers to the Maharajas in Delhi. Paul works with his nephew Master Punditt Joshi, travelling around the world visiting holy places in India and the Himalayas. Paul teaches advanced techniques of clairvoyance, healing and spiritual development to willing students. Paul relaxes listening to blues music with a good single malt whisky. He lives in the seaside town of Brighton on the south coast of England.

Paul's previous books are *The Tarot and the Magus* (Aeon Books, 2004) and *Beyond the Celtic Cross* (Aeon Books, 2009).

Paul can be found at any of the following sites:

tarocurrents.substack.com/
www.patreon.com/c/paulhughesbarlow
tarorota.co.uk/